Kubernetes Quick Start

Benjamin Young

Contents

1   Introduction   1

2   Kubernetes Basic Concepts   2

  2.1   Pod   2

  2.2   Node   3

  2.3   ReplicaSet   4

  2.4   Deployment   5

  2.5   Service   8

     2.5.1   ClusterIP service   8

     2.5.2   NodePort Service   10

     2.5.3   LoadBalancer   11

  2.6   Ingress and Ingress Controller   12

  2.7   StatefulSets   14

  2.8   DaemonSet   15

  2.9   Label and Selector   15

  2.10 YAML descriptor   16

3 Kubernetes installation   **19**

  3.1   K8s architecture 19

      3.1.1   control plane components: 20

      3.1.2   nodes components: 21

  3.2   install minikube 21

  3.3   install kind 21

  3.4   install K8s the hard way (on bare metal) 22

      3.4.1   prepare bare metal machine or virtual machine 22

      3.4.2   install container run-time on each node 23

      3.4.3   install kubelet kubeadm, kubectl on each node 25

      3.4.4   init on master/control plane node 25

      3.4.5   install pod network add-on on master node 27

      3.4.6   join other nodes to K8s cluster 27

      3.4.7   install K8s with swap on 27

      3.4.8   testing basic deployment, services 29

  3.5   install Load-balancer (MetalLB) 30

      3.5.1   what is namespace? 31

      3.5.2   testing load-balancer 33

  3.6   install Ingress (haproxy) 34

      3.6.1   testing ingress 35

  3.7   install Dashboard UI 36

  3.8   install HELM 40

4 Kubernetes Auto-scaling   **43**

  4.1   Horizontal Pod Autoscaler (HPA), Pods level Auto-scaling 43

      4.1.1   install metrics server 43

      4.1.2   testing HPA 44

  4.2   Cluster Autoscaler (CA) - Nodes level auto-scaling 47

      4.2.1   Overprovisioning 47

5 Storage   **49**

  5.1   volumes, volumeMounts 49

  5.2   PersistentVolume and PersistentVolumeClaim 50

  5.3   Storage Classes 50

  5.4   NFS storage classes example 52

      5.4.1   set up a NFS server 52

      5.4.2   install nfs-client provisioner using helm 53

      5.4.3   create a pvc using the storage class 54

      5.4.4   create a pod to use that pvc 55

6 Stateful Applications   **57**

  6.1   Deploy a stateful app using Deployment 57

  6.2   Deploy a stateful application using StatefulSet (cassandra) 58

      6.2.1   Create a Headless Service 58

      6.2.2   Create cassandra StatefulSets pod 59

      6.2.3   Ordered pod create and stable network identities 62

      6.2.4   Stable storage 64

      6.2.5   Access cassandra headless service from K8s node (inside K8s cluster) 65

      6.2.6   Access cassandra headless service from outside 65

      6.2.7   Cassandra quick start 66

      6.2.8   Scaling a StatefulSet 67

      6.2.9   Clean up a StatefulSet 68

7 Role-Based Access Control (RBAC)   **69**

  7.1   context vs namespace 70

  7.2   create a service account, role and rolebinding 71

  7.3   create a normal user account, role and rolebinding 71

      7.3.1   Create a new namespace and user credentials 71

      7.3.2   Create the role and rolebinding 73

      7.3.3   Testing the normal user using context 74

8   Misc   **76**

   8.1   Job   76

   8.2   CronJob   78

   8.3   ConfigMap   79

           8.3.1   Create ConfigMap   79

           8.3.2   Using ConfigMap   80

   8.4   Secrets   82

9   Cheat Sheet   **83**

   9.1   config related   83

   9.2   kubectl related   84

10 Index   **87**

List of Figures

2.1   multiple containers in a POD   3

2.2   multiple pods distributed on different nodes   4

2.3   multiples pods in ReplicaSet   5

2.4   deployment rolling-upgrade   7

2.5   service (ClusterIP)   9

2.6   Node Port service   11

2.7   LoadBalancer service   12

2.8   ingress   13

2.9   StatefulSets   14

3.1   K8s architecture   20

3.2   3-node bare metal home network   23

3.3   dashboard login   39

3.4   dashboard   40

5.1   volume, pv/pvc,storage class and its provisioner relationship   51

Benjamin Young is the owner of www.comnte.com, an information technology consulting firm based in Austin, TX, specialized in software development (machine/deep learning, voip, web development). He has more than 20 years experience in software engineering, system/network administration and has authored several books on docker, kubernetes, deep learning.

Do you want to understand key Kubernetes(K8s) jargons within several hours?
Do you want to know how to install K8s load-balancer, Ingress, Storage class in a bare metal environment?
Do you want to deploy your stateless/stateful application quickly?

Do you want to know how to auto-scaling your application effectively?

This book will help you learn and use kubernetes from scratch quickly and effectively using step by step practical examples.

In this book, you will learn:

* several key kubernetes concepts.
* how to install K8s cluster in a bare metal environment.
* how to auto-scaling your application.
* what is pv, pvc, storage class and how it works.
* how to deploy stateless/stateful applications
* How to use Role-Based Access Control (RBAC)

Kubernetes Quick Start

Benjamin Young

Copyright

For permission requests, email to author, at the address below:

benjamin@comrite.com

Web URL: http://www.comrite.com

Preface

Kubernetes (K8s) is an open-source system for automating deployment, scaling, and management of containerized applications. It is the de facto standard for container orchestration.

The learning curve is quite steep due to many concepts unique to k8s.

This book is an extended document based on my personal notes while learning k8s.

My goal is to help busy IT professionals to learn k8s as quickly as possible, but in a hard way, by setting up a bare metal k8s cluster in a typical home network, so that you have a solid K8s foundation to learn and use k8s later, for example, how to use K8s in AWS, Google cloud environment, etc.

The book does not intend to cover all K8s topics, but rather help you to jump start your K8s journey.

Readers should have some very basic knowledge of Linux/Unix, scripting, docker container, etc.

If you not familiar with docker container, as a shameless promotion, you can read my book at:
https://www.amazon.com/Docker-Dummies-world-Benjamin-Young-ebook/dp/B06Y295S49/

The source code of examples could be found at:

https://github.com/mingewang/kubernetes_quick_start

I welcome email from any readers with comments, suggestions, or bug fixes.

Benjamin Young

benjamin@comrite.com

June 2023

Disclaimer

Although the author and publisher have made every effort to ensure that the information in this book was correct at press time, the author and publisher do not assume and hereby disclaim any liability to any party for any loss, damage, or disruption caused by errors or omissions, whether such errors or omissions result from negligence, accident, or any other cause.

Acknowledgments

I would like to thank the invaluable support from my family for their patience while I worked late, often and sometimes on vacation.

Chapter 1

Introduction

Kubernetes was first announced by Google in mid-2014, and was heavily influenced by Google's Borg system.

It defines a set of building blocks that provide mechanisms to deploy, maintain, and scale applications based on CPU, memory or custom metrics.

The major obstacles to learn k8s are k8s's concepts.

Let's start.

Chapter 2

Kubernetes Basic Concepts

In this chapter, I will go over K8s's basic concepts, some of them are quite unique, some of them are quite confusing as they appear often in normal English sentences, but have their specific meaning from K8s point of view.

Tip
The content of those concepts does not mean to be complete here, as you can easily find those in the official k8s documents, instead, I will try to give you a brief high-level overview of those concepts, so you can get hold of those concepts.

2.1 Pod

Pod is a unique concept in k8s.

Roughly speaking, several tightly coupled containers (processes) can be put into a pod, and they share:

- A unique network IP

- Network

- Storage

- Any additional specifications that were applied to the pod.

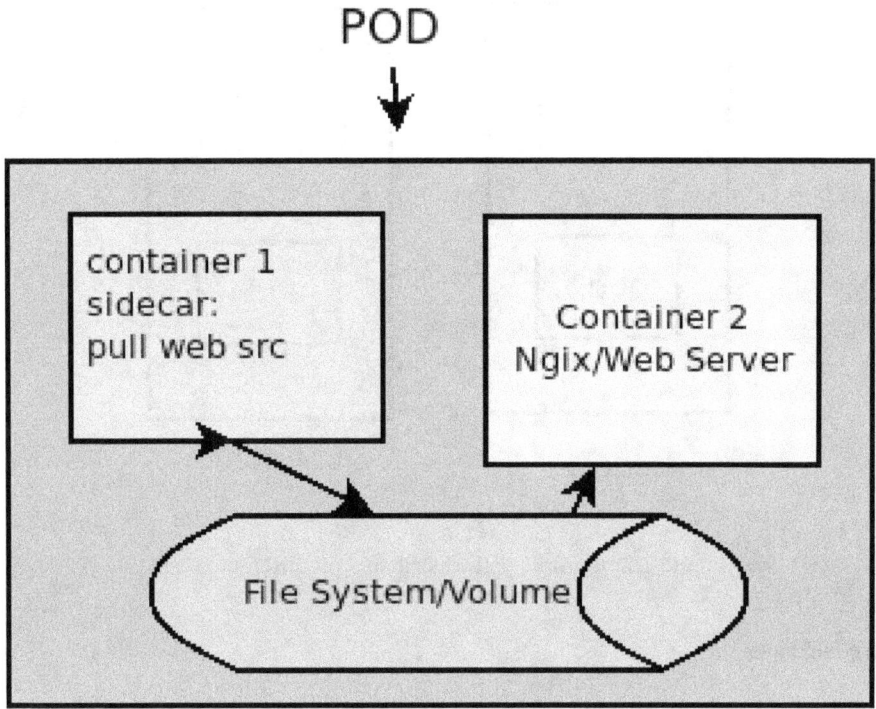

Figure 2.1: multiple containers in a POD

In another word, a pod can be thought as an application-specific **logical host**.

Pods are the **smallest deployable units** of computing that you can create and manage in Kubernetes.

More details at: https://kubernetes.io/docs/concepts/workloads/pods/

2.2   Node

Node is like a physical host, though it could be a bare metal machine or virtual machine. Its primary purpose is to host Pods, thus it will contains the services necessary to run Pods, managed by the control plane.

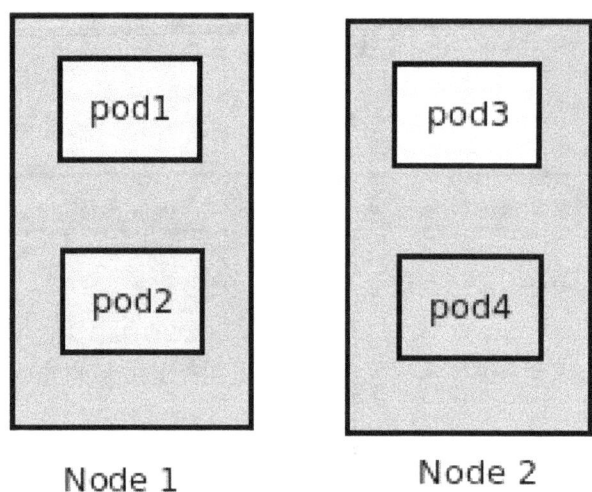

Figure 2.2: multiple pods distributed on different nodes

In short, a node could have:

- container runtime

- kubelet. (start,maintain pods etc)

- kube-proxy. (handle network request from control plane/master node)

- multiple pods.

2.3 ReplicaSet

As you can guess, it means multiple identical Pods running at the same time to guarantee the high availability.

For example, nginx pod1 can be run at node1, pod2 at node2, ... etc.

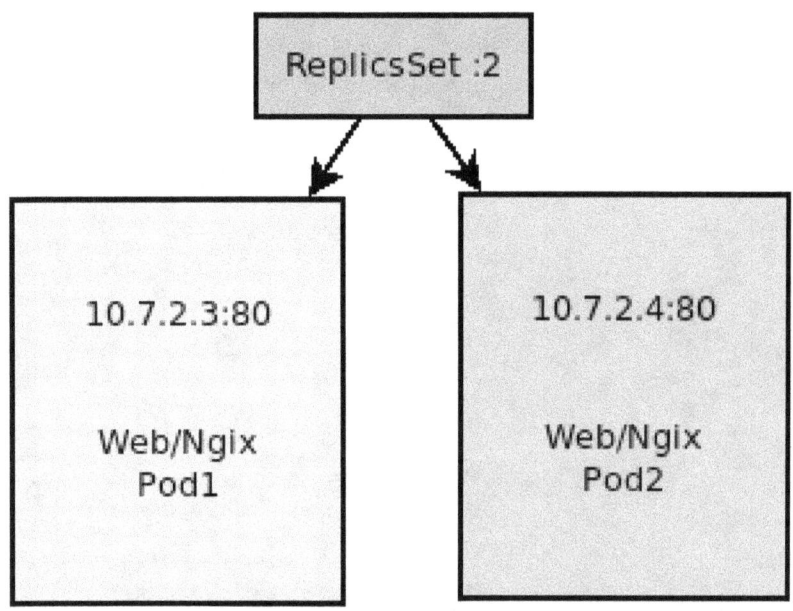

Figure 2.3: multiples pods in ReplicaSet

These replicas/pods don't differ from each other, apart from their name and IP address.

Normally we do not use ReplicaSets directly, instead we use Deployment to deploy the ReplicaSets.

2.4   Deployment

In k8s, the deployment is the standard way to deploy Pods ReplicaSets to nodes. We use a declarative yaml file to define a deployment, inside which we define replicas.

For example:

```
apiVersion: apps/v1
kind: Deployment
metadata:
 name: nginx-deployment
 labels:
```

```
    app: nginx
spec:
 replicas: 3                 <-- specify the number of replicas
 strategy:
   type: RollingUpdate
   rollingUpdate:
     maxSurge: 2            # how many pods we can add at a time
     maxUnavailable: 0     # maxUnavailable define how many pods can be unavailable
                            # during the rolling update
 selector:
   matchLabels:
     app: nginx
 template:
   metadata:
     labels:
       app: nginx
   spec:
     containers:
     - name: nginx
       image: nginx:1.14.2
       ports:
       - containerPort: 80
```

I will explain the yaml file in detail later.

One cool feature of deployment is it can also help us upgrade/roll-back pods automatically by defining RollingUp-dateStrategy inside that deployment file.

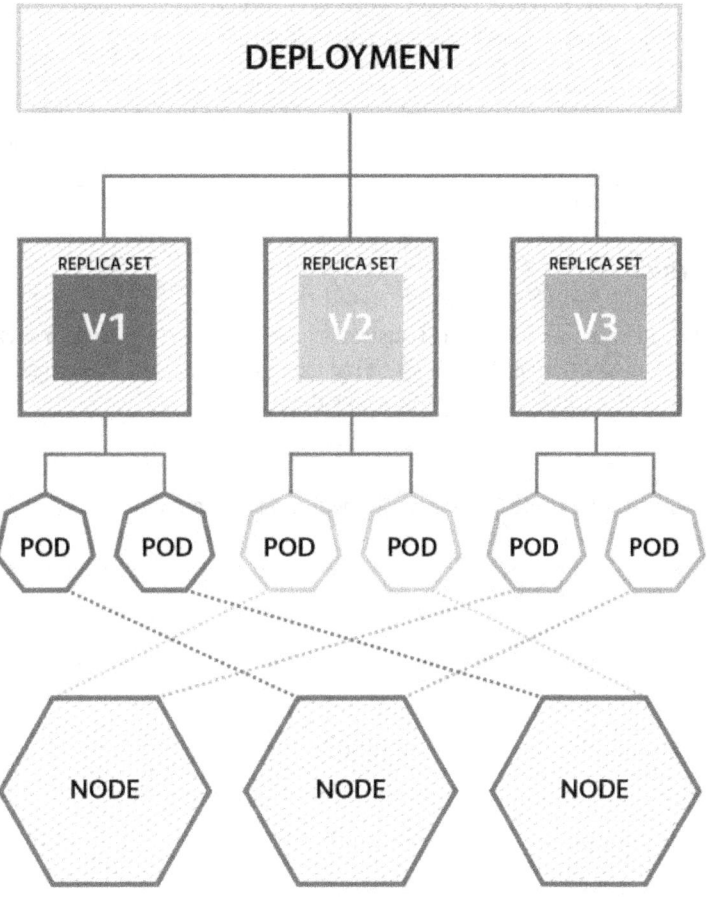

Figure 2.4: deployment rolling-upgrade

We will talk about this in more detail later.

2.5 Service

It exposes an application running on a set of Pods as a network service.

Tip
Those pods could be started by a Deployment or other means (e.g. StatefulSets that will be introduced later).

2.5.1 ClusterIP service

A typical service specifies the type of service as ClusterIP, making the service **only reachable from within the cluster**. K8s normally assigns an internal IP to this service from its service network ip address space. That means someone from outside the cluster can NOT access this service!

Tip
We can still access the service by using kubectl port-forward, but it is not normal, usually it is just for developer's use.

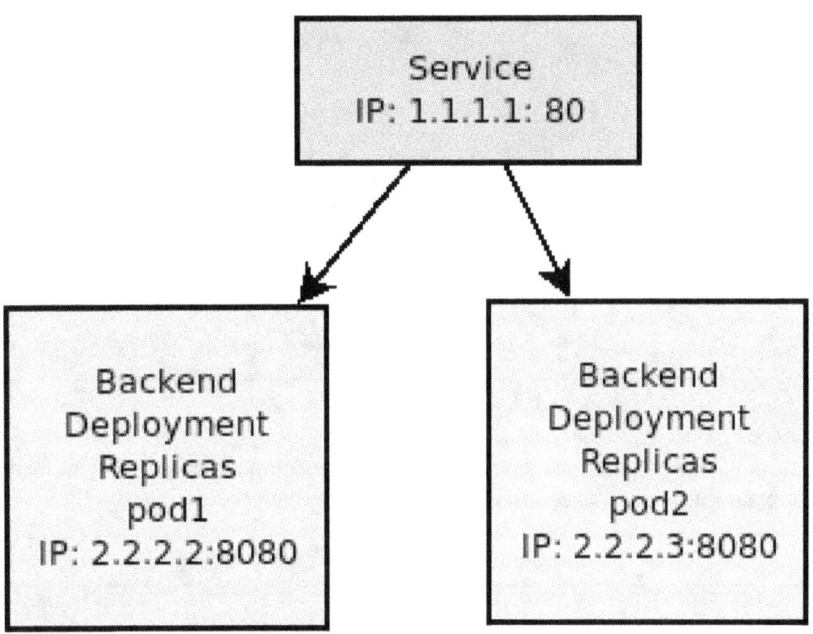

Figure 2.5: service (ClusterIP)

Tip

K8s usually assigns IP to its Pods from **Pods network address space** e.g: 10.32.0.0/24, and assigns IP to its service/ClusterIP from **((Service network address space))**, e.g: 10.96.0.0/24.

To expose the service to outside world, we have to use **LoadBalancer, NodePort, or Ingress**. To confuse you more, the LoadBalancer and NodePort are defined as "kind:services" in a k8s yaml file, while ingress is defined as "kind:Ingress".

The distinguish between regular service, NodePort, LoadBalancer is in **sepc.type**, see the following:

```
apiVersion: v1
kind: Service
metadata:
 name: example-service
spec:
```

```
selector:
  app: example
ports:
  - port: 8765
    targetPort: 9376
type: ClusterIP          <--- regular service, usually assign an internal
                         | cluster ip only accessible from pod network
#type: LoadBalancer      <---- loadbalancer, usually assign
#                        | an external accessible IP
#type: NodePort          <---- open the same port on all the nodes
```

Tip

can I deploy a service?

It is a confusing saying from a layman. The deployment and service has their special meanings in k8s. "deploy a service" is a just plain English sentence, do not confuse deploy with deployment!

 Warning

Deployment does not have a general meaning as normal English, in K8s, it just means to deploy ReplicasSets, not StatefulSets. Please see StatefulSets later.

2.5.2 NodePort Service

This seems to be a unique feature if you just start to learn K8s.

It exposes the Service on each Node's IP at a static port (the NodePort). A ClusterIP Service, to which the NodePort Service routes, is automatically created.

You'll be able to contact the NodePort Service, from outside the cluster, by requesting <NodeIP>:<NodePort>.

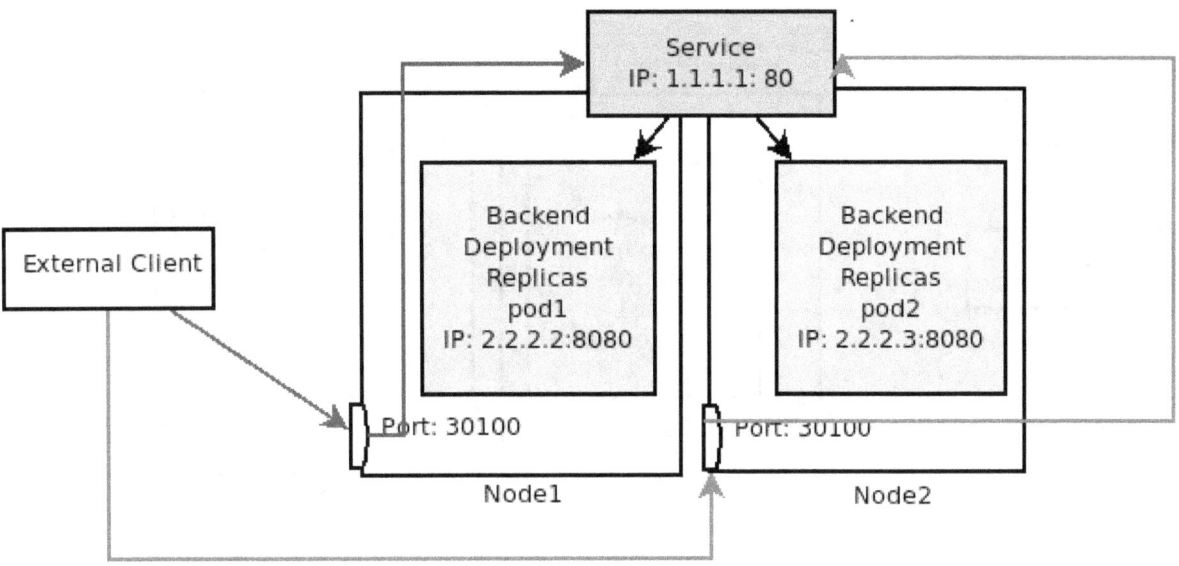

Figure 2.6: Node Port service

As shown in the diagram above, the external client can choose one of NodeIP:NodePort to send traffic, K8s will then route the traffic to its internal clusterIP service, which will in turn route the traffic to one of its pods.

2.5.3 LoadBalancer

As you see before, LoadBalancer exposes an application to the outside world, normally it means it will provide you a public accessible IP for this service etc.

Unlike a build-in out of box regular ClusterIP type of service from k8s, we usually **need to install a third-party load-balancer**, for example, MetalLB etc.

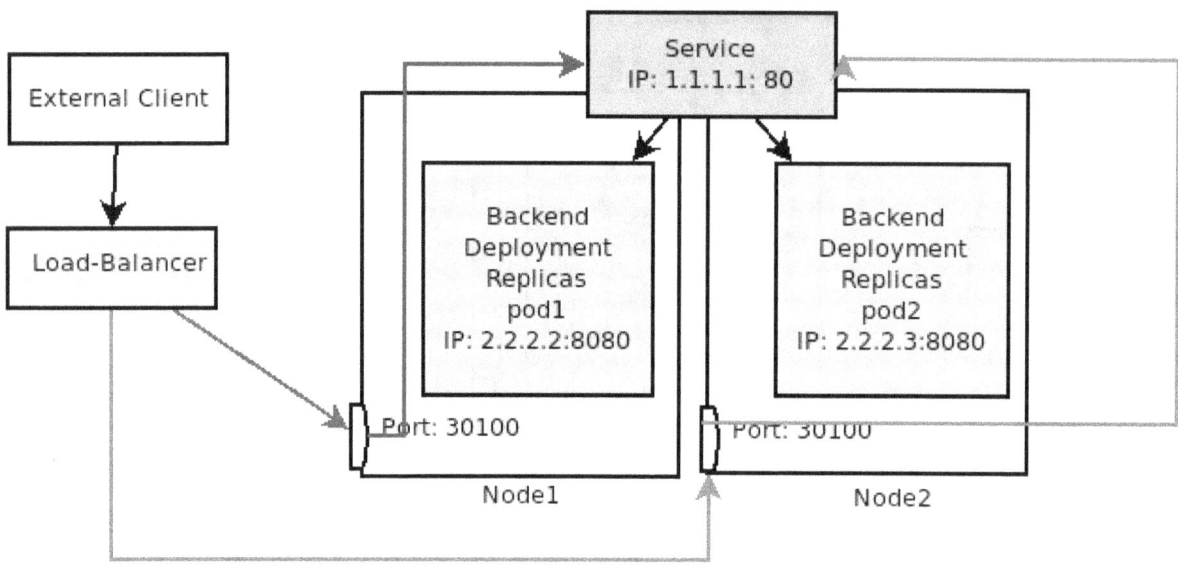

Figure 2.7: LoadBalancer service

The LoadBalancer will internally create NodePort and ClusterIP Services for us.

It works almost the same as NordPort except we let external client send traffic to the loadbalancer, which decides how to route the traffic to those NodePorts etc.

2.6   Ingress and Ingress Controller

Ingress manages external access to the services in a cluster, typically HTTP/HTTPS, actually only HTTP or HTTPS allowed in K8s's ingress.

The Ingress is an API object that defines rules which allow external access to services in a cluster, while an Ingress controller fulfills the rules set in the Ingress.

K8s does not provide any build-in Ingress controller, we need to install a third-party implementation: e.g. NGINX ingress controller, HAProxy Ingress controller etc.

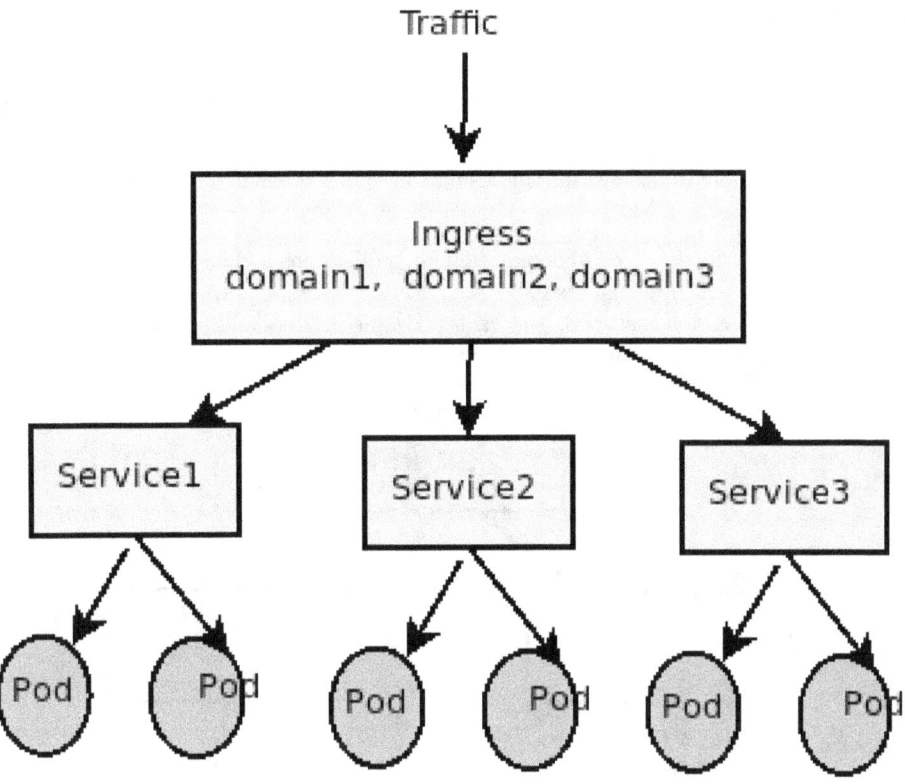

Figure 2.8: ingress

Tip

The difference between Load-balancer and Ingress is: load-balancer operates at layer 4, while Ingress operates at Layer 7. That means one load-balancer IP can only expose one service, while one ingress IP can expose several internal services.

In short, ingress may provide load balancing, SSL termination and name-based virtual hosting services at layer 7 to outsider.

2.7 StatefulSets

For ReplicasSet, those pods are meant to be stateless. To be more accurate, **stateless** here means they are independent from each other, and pods are homogeneous.

The Deployment is the right tool to manage those pods that are based on an identical container spec, and good for stateless applications.

On the contrary, **StatefulSets** are designed to deploy stateful applications and clustered applications that save data to persistent storage, For example applications like Kafka, MySQL, Redis, ZooKeeper etc need unique, persistent identities and stable hostnames for each pod, and each pod must be treated as non-fungible individuals. Such applications normally have one or more masters and multiple slaves.

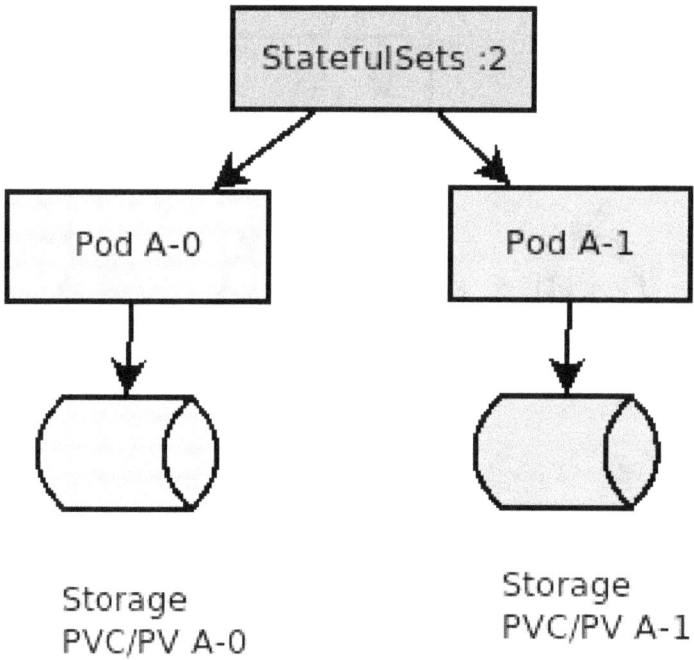

Figure 2.9: StatefulSets

StatefulSets provides similar functions as Deployment, in addition, it provides:

- Stable, unique network identifiers.
  For example, if it is ReplicaSet pod, k8s will give each pod some random name: A-rxd, A-sbf.
  But For StatefulSet pods, k8s will give each pod and ordinal index name for example: A-0, A-1, ... etc.
  If the pod A-0 gets killed, K8s will start another pod, but with the same name A-0.

- Stable, persistent storage.
  It means for each pod, it will provide a stable dedicated storage, and if a pod restarts, it will see the same storage.

- Ordered, graceful deployment and scaling.
  It means K8s will start pod A-0 first, then start pod A-1 etc.

- Ordered, automated rolling updates.

Tip
stable is synonymous with persistence across Pod (re)scheduling.

2.8   DaemonSet

A DaemonSet is relatively easy to understand.

In short, it ensures that all (or some) Nodes run a copy of a Pod. Some typical uses of a DaemonSet are:

- running a cluster storage daemon on every node

- running a logs collection daemon on every node

- running a node monitoring daemon on every node

...

As nodes are added to the cluster, Pods are added to them. As nodes are removed from the cluster, those Pods are garbage collected.

2.9   Label and Selector

Those two concepts are quite unique in K8s.

K8s is purposely designed to have no hierarchy, and all components are independent, but we need a way to describe relationships between two objects, thus labels and selectors play a key role to link/relate those objects together.

In short, labels are key/value pairs that are attached to K8s objects, and later we use label Selectors to match/filter those objects.

The following showed how to define labels:

```
// in yaml file, we can define labels:
metadata:
 labels:
   key1 : value1
   key2 : value2
```

The following showed how to use selectors:

```
// in yaml file, we can use selector, to select objects
selector:
   key1: value1
```

In K8s, there is another special selector called nodeSelector, which applies to how to select a node to run.

```
// in yaml file, we can use selector, to select objects
nodeSelector:
   key1: value1
```

2.10 YAML descriptor

We can use kubectl command line or yaml/json descriptor to create K8s objects/resources.

Defining yaml/json descriptors in files make life easier once you get that file, we can use the following command to create/update K8s resources.

```
kubectl apply -f ./demo.yaml
```

Let's look at a concrete example of a pod:

```
apiVersion: v1           <--- api version used for this file
kind: Pod                <--- type of k8s resource/obj
metadata:                <--- metadata about this pod
 name: label-demo
```

```
labels:                          <--- two labels defined!
    environment: production
    app: nginx
spec:                             <--- pod spec: container/storage etc
 containers:                      <--- container
 - name: nginx
    image: k8s.gcr.io/nginx      <--- image to be used
    ports:                       <--- ports to expose from the container
    - containerPort: 9376
    resources:                   <--- resource requirement
      requests:                  <--- minimum cpu requirement for this pod
        cpu: "250m"              <--- 1/4 vCPU/Core or hyperthread
      limits:                    <--- max upper usage for this pod
        cpu: "500m"              <--- 1/2 vCPU/Core or hyperthread
 nodeSelector:                   <--- node Selector: which node to use
    accelerator:gpu              <--- selector matching condition
```

Another example of service using the pods defined:

```
apiVersion: v1
kind: Service                     <--- type of k8s resource/obj
metadata:
 name: my-service
spec:
 selector:                       <--- associate this service with pod
    app: nginx                   <--- condition to match previous pod
 ports:                          <--- list of ports that are exposed by this service
    - protocol: TCP
      port: 80                   <--- The port that will be exposed by this service
      targetPort: 9376           <--- Number or name of the port to access
                                      on the pods targeted by the service
```

I tried to explain the meaning for each line. Hope you get some ideas.

One question is how to know those fields' names and meanings? The concrete answer is: they are defined in K8s API documents:

https://kubernetes.io/docs/reference/

https://kubernetes.io/docs/reference/generated/kubernetes-api/v1.19

For example, if we need to find what fields a pod expects, we can look at:

https://kubernetes.io/docs/reference/generated/kubernetes-api/v1.19/#pod-v1-core

However, personally, I found it is much easier to just google for a sample yaml file, start from there; If really needed, you can check those API documents.

Chapter 3

Kubernetes installation

Now we have all the basic knowledge of K8s, let's install it.

3.1   K8s architecture

The following shows what a minimum K8s cluster should look likes:

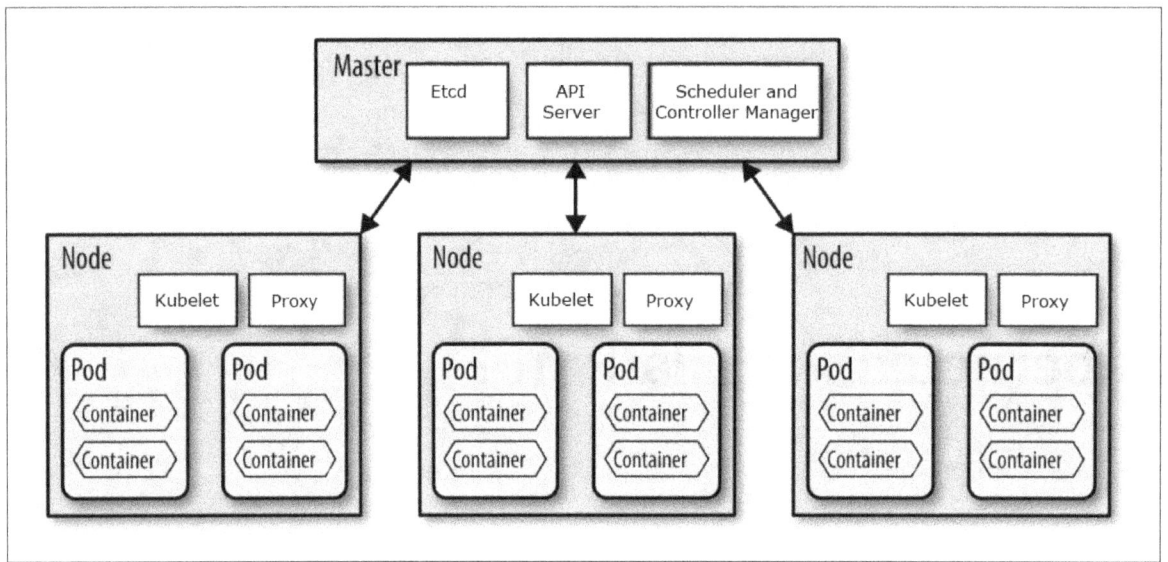

Figure 3.1: K8s architecture

3.1.1 control plane components:

- api-server: exposes K8s API. All interactions between components are through the API server.

- etcd: store all cluster/configure etc data.

- scheduler: watches pods with no-assigned nodes and selects a node for them to run on.
  notes: it does not really create pods!

- controller-manager: it has several controllers,

  - Node controller: Responsible for noticing and responding when nodes go down.

  - Replication controller: Responsible for maintaining the correct number of pods for every replication controller object in the system.

  - Endpoints controller: Populates the Endpoints object (that is, joins Services & Pods).

  - Service Account & Token controllers: Create default accounts and API access tokens for new namespaces.

– other controllers or third-party controllers.

Those components can be run on any machine in the cluster. However, for simplicity, set up scripts typically start all control plane components on the same machine, and do not run user containers on this machine.

3.1.2 nodes components:

One each node, there are:

- kubelet: takes a set of PodSpecs and ensures that the containers are running and healthy

- kube-proxy: a network proxy that implements part of the Kubernetes Service etc.

- container runtime: could be docker, containerd, CDR-O etc.

3.2 install minikube

According to K8s documents: Minikube is a tool that makes it easy to run Kubernetes locally. It runs a single-node Kubernetes cluster inside a Virtual Machine (VM) on your laptop for users looking to try out Kubernetes or develop with it day-to-day.

I will skip this as single-node K8s seems to be boring. You can read more details at:

https://kubernetes.io/docs/tasks/tools/install-minikube/

3.3 install kind

kind allows you to run **several-node K8s cluster on one single machine**, It uses Docker container "nodes", basically running K8s inside a container.

It is the quickest one to experiment with the K8s cluster.

You can find how to install at: https://kind.sigs.k8s.io/docs/user/quick-start/

Once it is installed, you can

```
kind create cluster  # create cluster

# normal kubectl commands

kubectl get nodes  #
kubectl get pods   #
...
```

3.4 install K8s the hard way (on bare metal)

I found it is more rewarding to install K8s on bare metal machine (or VM), it will give you a deeper understanding of how K8s works.

3.4.1 prepare bare metal machine or virtual machine

The first step is to prepare at least 3 bare-metal machines or VMs with basic OS on it.

One particular thing that needs to be aware of is: swap needs to be disabled.

Tip
Why swap off?
According to K8s developers: Support for swap is non-trivial. Guaranteed pods should never require swap. Burstable pods should have their requests met without requiring swap. BestEffort pods have no guarantee. The kubelet right now lacks the smarts to provide the right amount of predictable behavior here across pods.

Tip
There is workaround to not disable swap by passing **--fail-swap-on = false** to kubelet command line, or set **failSwapOn: false** to its config file at: /var/lib/kubelet/config.yaml

---

I used Debian/Linux 10 as the OS, you can choose any OS. The following notes apply to Debian, but should be applicable to other Linux-based OS any well.

And my internal network is a typical home network, plain flat network:

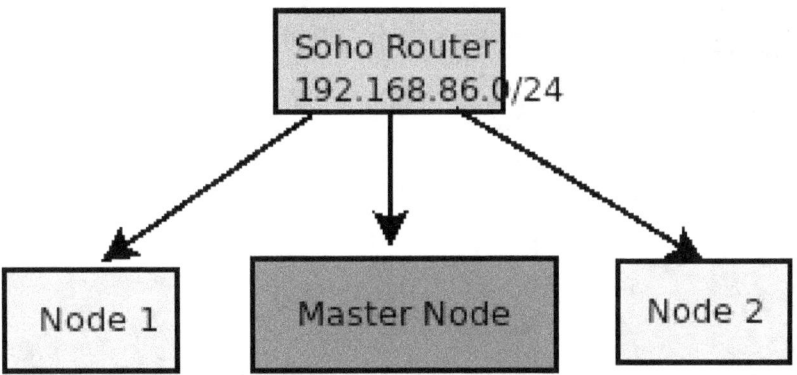

Figure 3.2: 3-node bare metal home network

3.4.2   install container run-time on each node

The k8s need container runtime on each node.

Since Kubernetes 1.27, k8s requires that you use a runtime that conforms with the Container Runtime Interface (CRI). Some popular CRI are:

- containerd

- CRI-O

- Docker Engine

- Mirantis Container Runtime

Here I installed the docker and containerd by following the instruction at:

https://docs.docker.com/engine/install/debian/

```
# prepare repo
$ sudo apt-get update
$ sudo apt-get install \
    apt-transport-https \
    ca-certificates \
    curl \
```

```
    gnupg-agent \
    software-properties-common

$ curl -fsSL https://download.docker.com/linux/debian/gpg | sudo apt-key add -

$ sudo add-apt-repository \
  "deb [arch=amd64] https://download.docker.com/linux/debian \
  $(lsb_release -cs) \
  stable"

# install docker and containerd
$ sudo apt-get update
$ sudo apt-get install docker-ce docker-ce-cli containerd.io

# need to update /etc/containerd/config.toml as following:

#disabled_plugins = ["cri"]
version = 2
[plugins."io.containerd.grpc.v1.cri".containerd.runtimes.runc]
  runtime_type = "io.containerd.runc.v2"
  [plugins."io.containerd.grpc.v1.cri".containerd.runtimes.runc.options]
    SystemdCgroup = true

# if you have private docker registry, you need this
# https://github.com/containerd/containerd/blob/main/docs/hosts.md
# https://github.com/containerd/cri/blob/master/docs/registry.md#configure- ↵
    registry-tls-communication
[plugins."io.containerd.grpc.v1.cri".registry]
  config_path = "/etc/containerd/certs.d"

# where the certs.d containers your registry's ca certs, e.g
certs.d/
certs.d/docker-eng.comrite.com:9443
certs.d/docker-eng.comrite.com:9443/ca.crt
certs.d/docker-eng.comrite.com
certs.d/docker-eng.comrite.com/ca.crt


$ sudo systemclt restart containerd
```

You can find install instruction for your OS at:

https://docs.docker.com/engine/install/

3.4.3   install kubelet kubeadm, kubectl on each node

The K8s installation is actually quite easy, just follow the instruction from:

https://kubernetes.io/docs/setup/production-environment/tools/kubeadm/install-kubeadm/

Here is mine:

```
# on each node:

cat <<EOF | sudo tee /etc/sysctl.d/k8s.conf
net.bridge.bridge-nf-call-ip6tables = 1
net.bridge.bridge-nf-call-iptables = 1
EOF
sudo sysctl --system

TIP: More details of docker runtime requirements for k8s:
https://kubernetes.io/docs/setup/production-environment/container-runtimes/


# prepare repo
sudo apt-get update && sudo apt-get install -y apt-transport-https curl
sudo mkdir -p /etc/apt/keyrings/
curl -fsSL https://packages.cloud.google.com/apt/doc/apt-key.gpg | sudo gpg -- ↩
    dearmor -o /etc/apt/keyrings/kubernetes-archive-keyring.gpg

echo "deb [signed-by=/etc/apt/keyrings/kubernetes-archive-keyring.gpg] https:// ↩
    apt.kubernetes.io/ kubernetes-xenial main" | sudo tee /etc/apt/sources.list.d ↩
    /kubernetes.list


# install K8s
sudo apt-get update
sudo apt-get install -y kubelet kubeadm kubectl

#hold - this option used to mark a package as held back,
#which will block the package from being installed, upgraded or removed
sudo apt-mark hold kubelet kubeadm kubectl
```

3.4.4   init on master/control plane node

Now at this stage, you can choose one node as your master node.

```
sudo kubeadm init
```

It took a while, maybe a couple of minutes.

You should see a similar output as following:

```
[kubelet-finalize] Updating "/etc/kubernetes/kubelet.conf"
to point to a rotatable kubelet client certificate and key
[addons] Applied essential addon: CoreDNS
[addons] Applied essential addon: kube-proxy

Your Kubernetes control-plane has initialized successfully!

To start using your cluster, you need to run the following as a regular user:

  mkdir -p $HOME/.kube
  sudo cp -i /etc/kubernetes/admin.conf $HOME/.kube/config
  sudo chown $(id -u):$(id -g) $HOME/.kube/config

You should now deploy a pod network to the cluster.
Run "kubectl apply -f [podnetwork].yaml" with one of the options listed at:
  https://kubernetes.io/docs/concepts/cluster-administration/addons/

Then you can join any number of worker nodes by running the following on each as  ↩
    root:

kubeadm join 192.168.86.30:6443 --token yql9dw.0nm7droics8ysqx6 \
    --discovery-token-ca-cert-hash \
      sha256:94a100792141e445ab4dc1133636280ae51f13667011d86756afb8d938a5f585
```

Following the instruction, we need to do it as a regular user (not root)

```
mkdir -p $HOME/.kube
sudo cp -i /etc/kubernetes/admin.conf $HOME/.kube/config
sudo chown $(id -u):$(id -g) $HOME/.kube/config
```

Tip

You can use "kubeadm reset" to restart again the init process. You can use "kubeadm token create --print-join-command" to show the join token.

3.4.5   install pod network add-on on master node

The previous instruction told us to deploy a pod network at:

https://kubernetes.io/docs/concepts/cluster-administration/addons/

There are many options, I chose wavenet here.

Tip

Which CNI (container network interface) to choose? You can read more at:

https://rancher.com/blog/2019/2019-03-21-comparing-kubernetes-cni-providers-flannel-calico-canal-and-weave/

```
# install wavenet
kubectl apply -f "https://cloud.weave.works/k8s/net?k8s-version=$(kubectl version ↩
    | base64 | tr -d '\n'
```

3.4.6   join other nodes to K8s cluster

Now we can join other nodes to this cluster by simply running the following command on that node:

```
kubeadm join 192.168.86.30:6443 --token yql9dw.0nm7droics8ysqx6 \
    --discovery-token-ca-cert-hash \
    sha256:94a100792141e445ab4dc1133636280ae51f13667011d86756afb8d938a5f585
```

By default, K8s cluster will not schedule Pods on the control-plane node for security reasons. But our testing cluster with limited nodes, we want to be able to schedule Pods on the control-plane node as well, so we can do:

```
kubectl taint node --all node-role.kubernetes.io/control-plane:NoSchedule-
```

3.4.7   install K8s with swap on

Sometimes you may have an old system that do not want to disable swap. It is still possible to install K8s.

You can try this:

```
# on master node as root
# turn off swap first
sudo swapoff -a
#
sudo kubeadm init

#after this , we can add
failSwapOn: false
to /var/lib/kubelet/config.yaml

# turn on swap
sudo swapon -a

sudo systemctl daemon-reload
sudo systemctl restart kubelet
```

On the other nodes (swap on),

```
# you can do
kubeadm join 192.168.86.30:6443 --token yql9dw.0nm7droics8ysqx6    \
--discovery-token-ca-cert-hash \
  sha256:94a100792141e445ab4dc1133636280ae51f13667011d86756afb8d938a5f585 \
 --ignore-preflight-errors=Swap

# it could failed, at this time
# we can add
failSwapOn: false
to /var/lib/kubelet/config.yaml

# then do the kubeadm join again, this time should work
kubeadm join 192.168.86.30:6443 --token yql9dw.0nm7droics8ysqx6    \
--discovery-token-ca-cert-hash \
  sha256:94a100792141e445ab4dc1133636280ae51f13667011d86756afb8d938a5f585 \
 --ignore-preflight-errors=Swap
```

Warning
You are warned that it is **not recommended** from K8s at all. I have installed K8s with "swap on" successfully on my local setup, and just let it run for a while, it seems to be ok. Then I turned-off the swap to avoid unpleasant surprises. You are at your own risk if you run K8s with swap-on.

3.4.8   testing basic deployment, services

Let's create a deployment and service.

```
$ cat php-apache.yaml
apiVersion: apps/v1
kind: Deployment
metadata:
  name: php-apache
spec:
  selector:
    matchLabels:
      run: php-apache
  replicas: 1
  template:
    metadata:
      labels:
        run: php-apache
    spec:
      containers:
      - name: php-apache
        image: k8s.gcr.io/hpa-example
        ports:
        - containerPort: 80
        resources:
          limits:
            cpu: 500m
          requests:
            cpu: 200m
---
apiVersion: v1
kind: Service
metadata:
  name: php-apache
  labels:
    run: php-apache
spec:
  ports:
  - port: 80
  selector:
    run: php-apache

# apply it
```

```
$ kubectl apply -f php-apache.yaml

# let's check it
$ kubectl get pods
NAME                           READY    STATUS     RESTARTS    AGE
php-apache-d4cf67d68-7fgx2     1/1      Running    0           4d9h

$ kubectl get deployment
NAME         READY    UP-TO-DATE    AVAILABLE    AGE
php-apache   1/1      1             1            4d23h

# let's check its service
$ kubectl get service
NAME         TYPE         CLUSTER-IP       EXTERNAL-IP    PORT(S)    AGE
php-apache   ClusterIP    10.98.239.222    <none>         80/TCP     4d23h

$ curl 10.98.239.222
OK

# on any other machine ( not in this cluster, meaning not those nodes )
$ curl 10.98.239.222
... <--- timeout
```

That verifies that our cluster is working!

3.5   install Load-balancer (MetalLB)

Remember we need to install a third-party load-balancer in order to access the service from outside the cluster.

MetalLB's load-balancer is used here, I mainly followed this:

https://opensource.com/article/20/7/homelab-metallb

https://metallb.universe.tf/installation/

```
# Install load-balance
kubectl apply -f https://raw.githubusercontent.com/metallb/metallb/v0.9.3/ ↩
   manifests/namespace.yaml
kubectl apply -f https://raw.githubusercontent.com/metallb/metallb/v0.13.10/ ↩
   config/manifests/metallb-native.yaml
kubectl create secret generic -n metallb-system memberlist --from-literal= ↩
   secretkey="$(openssl rand -base64 128)"
```

I configured my home router's DHCP server to only assign IP from 192.168.86.100-255, so I know my 192.168.86.1-99 is free to use.

Thus here is my configure for MetalLB:

```
# cat config_map.yaml
apiVersion: metallb.io/v1beta1
kind: IPAddressPool
metadata:
  name: config
  namespace: metallb-system
spec:
  addresses:
  - 192.168.86.80-192.168.86.99
---
apiVersion: metallb.io/v1beta1
kind: L2Advertisement
metadata:
  name: l2-config
  namespace: metallb-system
```

Note: metalLB accepts subnet/mask format as well, e.g: 192.168.2.128/25

```
kubectl apply -f ./config_map.yaml
```

Now we should be able to use a load-balancer.

3.5.1   what is namespace?

K8s supports multiple virtual clusters backed by the same physical cluster. These virtual clusters are called namespaces. It is a way to divide cluster resources between multiple users.

Generally we can pass -n name-space_name to kubectl for certain commands. To list all resources in all namespaces, you can pass — all-namespaces.

For example

```
$ kubectl get namespace
NAME                 STATUS    AGE
default              Active    4d23h
ingress-controller   Active    2d9h
kube-node-lease      Active    4d23h
```

```
kube-public               Active   4d23h
kube-system               Active   4d23h      <--- kube system core system
kube-verify               Active   4d8h       <--- our testing for lb
kubernetes-dashboard      Active   4d
metallb-system            Active   4d8h       <--- metallb

# list pods in kube-system namespace
$ kubectl get pods -n kube-system
NAME                                READY   STATUS    RESTARTS   AGE
coredns-f9fd979d6-bkr5w             1/1     Running   0          4d23h
coredns-f9fd979d6-tkdlp             1/1     Running   0          4d23h
etcd-mailsrv                        1/1     Running   0          4d23h
kube-apiserver-mailsrv              1/1     Running   0          4d23h
kube-controller-manager-mailsrv     1/1     Running   0          4d23h
kube-proxy-rx84j                    1/1     Running   2          4d23h
kube-proxy-stcrm                    1/1     Running   0          4d9h
kube-proxy-t5njr                    1/1     Running   0          4d23h
kube-scheduler-mailsrv              1/1     Running   0          4d23h
metrics-server-6f698fc777-dnsh5     1/1     Running   0          4d10h
tiller-deploy-6fd89dcdc6-zl5hc      1/1     Running   0          11h
weave-net-n6sj2                     2/2     Running   0          4d9h
weave-net-qmxq8                     2/2     Running   0          4d22h
weave-net-xm8ck                     2/2     Running   7          4d22

# list all deployments in all namespaces
$ kubectl get deployment --all-namespaces
NAMESPACE                 NAME                        READY   UP-TO-DATE   AVAILABLE  <--
        AGE
default                   nginx                       1/1     1            1   <--
                2d9h
default                   php-apache                  1/1     1            1   <--
                4d22h
kube-system               coredns                     2/2     2            2   <--
                4d23h
kube-system               metrics-server              1/1     1            1   <--
                4d22h
kube-system               tiller-deploy               1/1     1            1   <--
                11h
kube-verify               kube-verify                 2/2     2            2   <--
                4d8h
kubernetes-dashboard      dashboard-metrics-scraper   1/1     1            1   <--
                4d
```

```
kubernetes-dashboard    kubernetes-dashboard      1/1      1          1  ↩
               4d
metallb-system          controller                1/1      1          1  ↩
               4d8h
```

3.5.2   testing load-balancer

First let's create a namespace and a deployment in that namespace, the purpose of namespace here is just to separate the testing service from our regular service.

```
# Create a new namespace
$ kubectl create namespace kube-verify

# create a deployment
$ cat <<EOF | kubectl create -f -
apiVersion: apps/v1
kind: Deployment
metadata:
  name: kube-verify
  namespace: kube-verify
  labels:
    app: kube-verify
spec:
  replicas: 3
  selector:
    matchLabels:
      app: kube-verify
  template:
    metadata:
      labels:
        app: kube-verify
    spec:
      containers:
      - name: nginx
        image: quay.io/clcollins/kube-verify:01
        ports:
        - containerPort: 80
EOF
```

Then let's create a lb yam file: verify_lb.yaml

```
apiVersion: v1
kind: Service
metadata:
  name: kube-verify
  namespace: kube-verify
spec:
  selector:
    app: kube-verify
  ports:
    - protocol: TCP
      port: 80
      targetPort: 80
  type: LoadBalancer     <--- this is what we need!
```

Then apply it by:

```
$ kubectl apply -f ./verify_lb.yaml
```

We can verify it:

```
# let's check which ip get assigned
$ kubectl get service -n kube-verify
NAME            TYPE           CLUSTER-IP      EXTERNAL-IP     PORT(S)        AGE
kube-verify     LoadBalancer   10.98.162.78    192.168.86.80   80:32323/TCP   4d7h


# test to access the service
# curl http://192.168.86.80
OK!
```

It is working!

3.6   install Ingress (haproxy)

K8s site list many Ingress controllers:

https://kubernetes.io/docs/concepts/services-networking/ingress-controllers/

I chose haproxy here for its simplicity and high performance.

I mainly followed its installation instruction at: https://haproxy-ingress.github.io/docs/getting-started/

```
# install haproxy ingress
$ kubectl create -f https://haproxy-ingress.github.io/resources/haproxy-ingress. ←
    yaml

# $ kubectl get nodes
NAME            STATUS    ROLES     AGE       VERSION
mailsrv         Ready     master    5d        v1.19.0    <-- my master node
ads             Ready     <none>    4d23h     v1.19.0
openstack01     Ready     <none>    4d9h      v1.19.0

# mark one of them as ingress-controller
# you can access the ingress using that node's ip
$ kubectl label node mailsrv role=ingress-controller

# actually you can label multiple node to be ingress-controller
#$ kubectl label node openstack01 role=ingress-controller


# after a while, check daemonsets and pods
$ kubectl get daemonsets -n ingress-controller
NAME                DESIRED   CURRENT   READY     UP-TO-DATE   AVAILABLE   NODE   ←
    SELECTOR          AGE
haproxy-ingress     1         1         1         1            1          role= ←
    ingress-controller   2d10h

$ kubectl get pods -n ingress-controller
NAME                READY     STATUS    RESTARTS   AGE
haproxy-ingress-m4dk4   1/1   Running   0          2d9h
```

Now ingress should work.

3.6.1   testing ingress

We will create a simple nginx service, and use ingress to route the traffic.

The ingress usually needs a valid DNS name in order to do the host-based http routing. Instead of mess our /etc/hosts, we can use nip.io (https://nip.io/), which is is a convenient service which converts a valid domain name to any IP, either public or local.

The DNS should point to the IP of that node with "role=ingress-controller", in my case: 192.168.86.30.

```
# create deployment
kubectl create deployment nginx --image nginx:alpine
# create a service
kubectl expose deployment nginx --port=80

# create haproxy ingress
$ more haproxy_ingress.yaml
apiVersion: extensions/v1beta1
kind: Ingress                                    <-- ingress !
metadata:
  name: nginx
spec:
  rules:
  - host: nginx.192.168.86.30.nip.io             <-- virtual host one
    http:
      paths:
      - backend:
          serviceName: nginx
          servicePort: 80
        path: /
  - host: php-apache.192.168.86.30.nip.io    <-- another virtual host
    http:
      paths:
      - backend:
          serviceName: php-apache
          servicePort: 80
        path: /

$ kubectl apply -f ./haproxy_ingress.yaml
```

Now on your browser, you should be able to access:

http://nginx.192.168.86.30.nip.io

and

http://php-apache.192.168.86.30.nip.io

3.7   install Dashboard UI

Now let's install K8s dashboard web ui.

The instruction is at: https://kubernetes.io/docs/tasks/access-application-cluster/web-ui-dashboard/

```
kubectl apply -f https://raw.githubusercontent.com/kubernetes/dashboard/v2.7.0/ ↩
    aio/deploy/recommended.yaml

kubectl get service -n kubernetes-dashboard

NAME                        TYPE        CLUSTER-IP       EXTERNAL-IP   PORT(S)      ↩
    AGE
dashboard-metrics-scraper   ClusterIP   10.102.113.84    <none>        8000/TCP     ↩
    5d
kubernetes-dashboard        ClusterIP   10.110.168.64    <none>        443/TCP      ↩
    5s
```

At this moment, if you have the config file from previous install and have kubectl installed on your machine, you can:

```
export KUBECONFIG="~/.kube/config"
kubectl proxy

Then access it at:
http://localhost:8001/api/v1/namespaces/kubernetes-dashboard/services/https: ↩
    kubernetes-dashboard:/proxy/#/login
```

It is not convenient at all.

So let's use our loadbalancer.

```
$ kubectl edit  service kubernetes-dashboard -n kubernetes-dashboard

# change
type: ClusterIP --> type: LoadBalancer

$ kubectl get services  -n kubernetes-dashboard
(base) mwang@mailsrv:~$ kubectl get services  -n kubernetes-dashboard
NAME          TYPE           CLUSTER-IP       EXTERNAL-IP      PORT(S)         AGE
kubernetes    LoadBalancer   10.110.168.64    192.168.86.81    443:32043/TCP   19m
-dashboard

# now we see it has external-ip!
# chrome somehow is very strict on ssl certificate, can not access it
# fortunately, we can use firefox to access it at:
# https://192.168.86.81
```

In order to access it, we need a token. Here is the quick start on how to create one:

https://www.replex.io/blog/how-to-install-access-and-add-heapster-metrics-to-the-kubernetes-dashboard

```
# create a service account
$ kubectl create serviceaccount dashboard-admin-sa

# bind the dashboard-admin-service-account service account to the cluster-admin ↵
    role
$ kubectl create clusterrolebinding dashboard-admin-sa --clusterrole=cluster- ↵
    admin \
    --serviceaccount=default:dashboard-admin-sa

# create long-lived API token
$ kubectl apply -f - <<EOF
apiVersion: v1
kind: Secret
metadata:
  name: dashboard-admin-sa
  annotations:
    kubernetes.io/service-account.name: dashboard-admin-sa
type: kubernetes.io/service-account-token
EOF

$ kubectl get secret/dashboard-admin-sa -o yaml

or
# let's get access-token from that secret
$ kubectl describe secret/dashboard-admin-sa
Name:           dashboard-admin-sa
Namespace:      default
Labels:         <none>
Annotations:    kubernetes.io/service-account.name: dashboard-admin-sa
                kubernetes.io/service-account.uid: 8c6f3ed5-96fd-44dc-a7c1-5511 ↵
                    a792a31e

Type:  kubernetes.io/service-account-token

Data
====
ca.crt:         1099 bytes
namespace:      7 bytes
token:          eyJhbGciOiJ... <-- copy/paste your token here
```

Copy/paste the token to your web-gui token

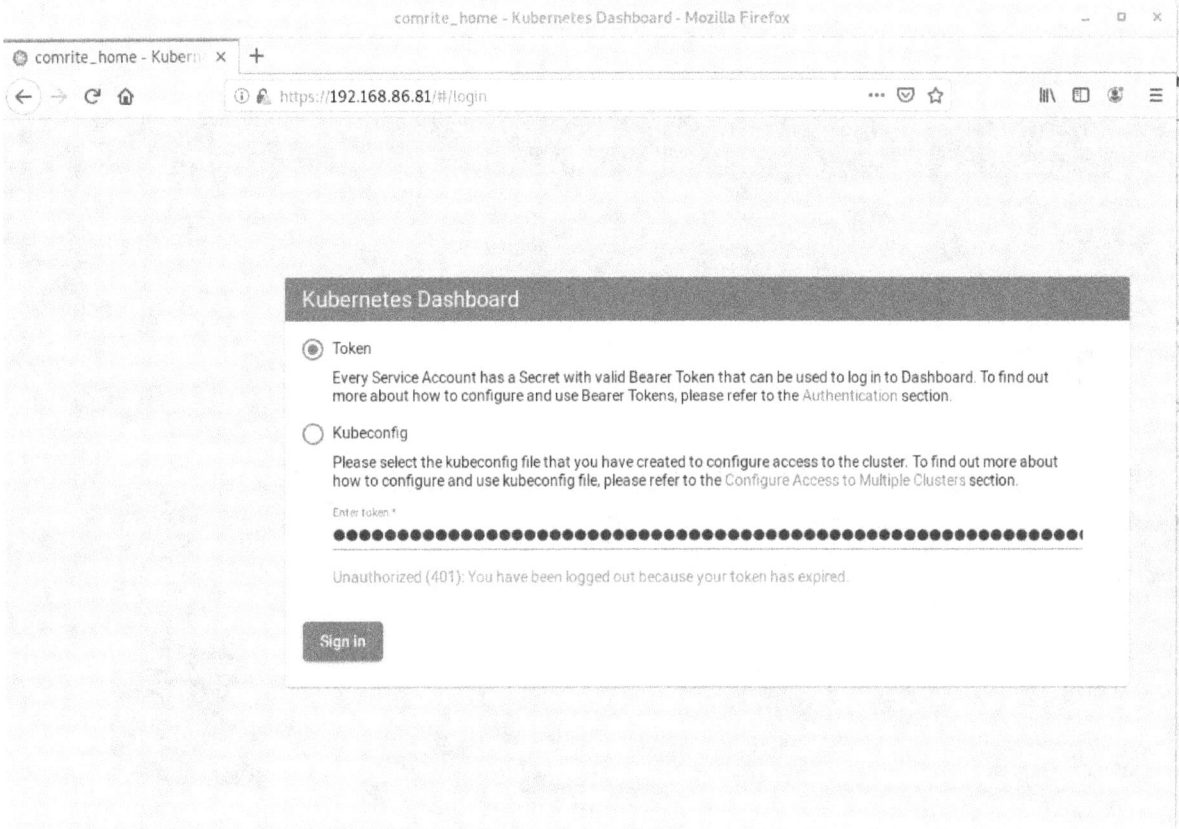

Figure 3.3: dashboard login

You should see this:

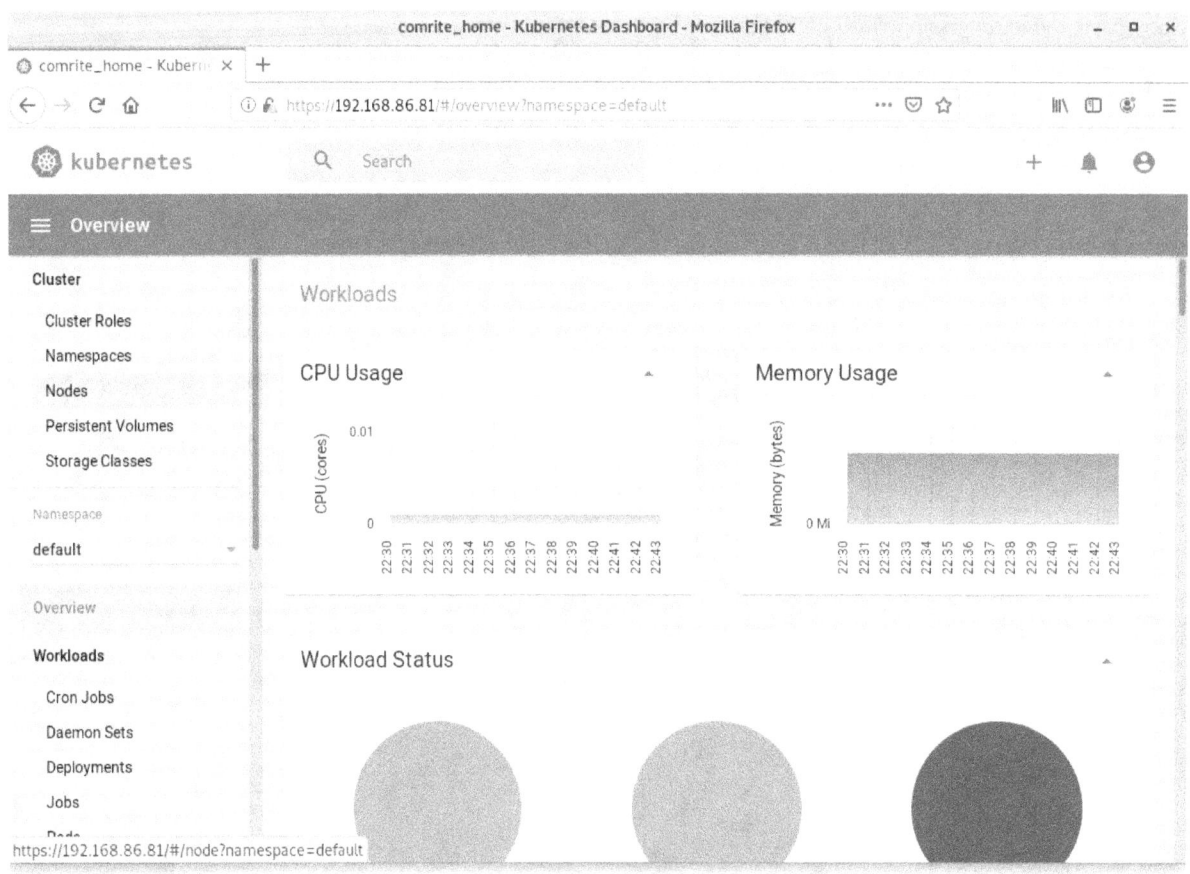

Figure 3.4: dashboard

3.8 install HELM

Writing K8s yaml file to deploy applications is not that fun considering the complexities of K8s.

Helm is created to help us to define, install, and upgrade even the most complex Kubernetes application.

It packages an K8s application's installation/configure into an chart, which contains all of the resource definitions necessary to run an application, tool, or service inside of a K8s cluster.

You can search/install/uninstall just like those other package managers: apt for debian, yum for Redhat etc.

First let's install it. I just followed the instruction at:

https://helm.sh/docs/intro/install/

```
curl https://baltocdn.com/helm/signing.asc | sudo apt-key add -
sudo apt-get install apt-transport-https --yes
echo "deb https://baltocdn.com/helm/stable/debian/ all main"
| sudo tee /etc/apt/sources.list.d/helm-stable-debian.list
sudo apt-get update
sudo apt-get install helm
```

Let's use it.

```
# add repo called stable
$ helm repo add stable https://charts.helm.sh/stable

# list repo
$ helm repo list
NAME              URL
stable            https://kubernetes-charts.storage.googleapis.com/
descheduler       https://kubernetes-sigs.github.io/descheduler/

# search repo
$ helm search repo mysql
NAME                    CHART VERSION    APP VERSION      DESCRIPTION
stable/mysql            1.6.7            5.7.30           Fast, reliable, scalable, ↩
    ..
stable/mysqldump        2.6.1            2.4.1            A Helm chart to help  ↩
    backup MySQL ..

# search helm chart ( online )
$ helm search hub mysql
(base) mwang@mailsrv:~$ helm search hub mysql
URL                                       CHART VERSION    APP VERSION       ↩
    DESCRIPTIOn
https://hub.helm.sh/charts/inspur/dble    0.0.2            2.19.09           DBLE is a
                                          high scalability middle-ware for MySQ...


$ helm repo update                # Make sure we get the latest list of charts
$ helm install stable/mysql --generate-name
Released smiling-penguin
```

```
$ helm uninstall smiling-penguin
Removed smiling-penguin
```

There are many free applications/charts online.

Chapter 4

Kubernetes Auto-scaling

The very cool and useful feature of K8s is its auto-scaling. There are pod-level auto-scaling, and node-level auto-scaling.

4.1 Horizontal Pod Autoscaler (HPA), Pods level Auto-scaling

HPA automatically scales the number of pods in a replication controller, deployment, replica set or stateful set based on observed CPU utilization (or, with beta support, on some other, application-provided metrics).

4.1.1 install metrics server

In order for HPA to work, first we need to install K8s metrics server, which collects resource metrics from Kubelets and exposes them in K8s apiserver through Metrics API for use by Horizontal Pod Autoscaler and Vertical Pod Autoscaler. Metrics API can also be accessed by kubectl top, making it easier to debug autoscaling pipelines.

The install instruction is at: https://github.com/kubernetes-sigs/metrics-server

Somehow not working, so I have to do this:

```
# download the components
$ kubectl apply -f https://github.com/kubernetes-sigs/metrics-server/releases/ ↵
    latest/download/components.yaml
```

```
# install it
$ kubectl apply -f components.yaml


# check/verify
$ kubectl get svc -n kube-system
NAME            TYPE      CLUSTER-IP    EXTERNAL-IP  PORT(S)                  AGE
kube-dns        ClusterIP 10.96.0.10    <none>       53/UDP,53/TCP,9153/TCP   7d
metrics-server  ClusterIP 10.101.3.105<none>         443/TCP                  6d23h

# we can see who is the top node/pod now!
$ kubectl top nodes
NAME          CPU(cores)   CPU%     MEMORY(bytes)    MEMORY%
ads           287m         4%       2956Mi           88%
mailsrv       279m         6%       2409Mi           30%
openstack01   98m          1%       1277Mi           16%


$ kubectl top pods
NAME                            CPU(cores)     MEMORY(bytes)
nginx-565785f75c-bfqtl          0m             9Mi
php-apache-d4cf67d68-7fgx2      1m             15Mi


$ kubectl top pod -n kube-sytsem
NAME                            CPU(cores)     MEMORY(bytes)
coredns-f9fd979d6-bkr5w         5m             13Mi
coredns-f9fd979d6-tkdlp         5m             12Mi
etcd-mailsrv                    32m            58Mi
...

# list top containers inside this pod
$ kubectl top pod etcd-mailsrv -n kube-system --containers

# list top pod with that label
$  kubectl top pod -l app=test
```

https://www.datadoghq.com/blog/how-to-collect-and-graph-kubernetes-metrics/

4.1.2   testing HPA

With metrics server in-place, we can try HPA now!

I mainly follow this:

https://kubernetes.io/docs/tasks/run-application/horizontal-pod-autoscale-walkthrough/

Enabling HPA on a deployment is extremely easy:

```
# create deployment
$ kubectl apply -f https://k8s.io/examples/application/php-apache.yaml

# enable HPA!
$ kubectl autoscale deployment php-apache --cpu-percent=50 --min=1 --max=10

# now check it, it is enabled!
$ kubectl get hpa
NAME          REFERENCE            TARGETS   MINPODS   MAXPODS   REPLICAS   AGE
php-apache    Deployment/php-apache 0%/50%   1         10        1          6 ↩
    d23h
```

Now testing is with heavy load:

```
kubectl run -it --rm load-generator --image=busybox /bin/sh
Hit enter for command prompt
while true; do wget -q -O- http://php-apache; done
```

Within a minute or so, we should see the higher CPU load by executing:

```
$ kubectl get hpa
NAME          REFERENCE      TARGET       MINPODS   MAXPODS   REPLICAS   AGE
php-apache    Deployment
              /php-apache/scale  305% / 50%  1        10         1          3m

# CPU consumption has increased to 305% of the request.
# As a result, the deployment was resized to 7 replicas:
$kubectl get deployment php-apache
NAME          READY   UP-TO-DATE   AVAILABLE   AGE
php-apache    7/7     7            7           19m
```

If we kill/exit the previous pod, after a while, the HPA will reduce the pods.

```
$ kubectl get hpa
NAME          REFERENCE      TARGETS   MINPODS   MAXPODS   REPLICAS   AGE
php-apache    Deployment
              /php-apache    0%/50%    1         10        1          6d23h
```

```
# how what resources/limits pods requested on a node
$ kubectl describe node mailsrv
..
Non-terminated Pods:           (13 in total)
Namespace   Name      CPU Requests CPU Limits Memory Requests Memory Limits AGE
ingress     haproxy-  0 (0%)       0 (0%)     0 (0%)          0 (0%)        10
controller ingress-m4kk4
...


Allocated resources:
  (Total limits may be over 100 percent, i.e., overcommitted.)
  Resource           Requests        Limits
  --------           --------        ------
  cpu                1450m (36%)     600m (15%)
  memory             1464Mi (18%)    1464Mi (18%)
  ephemeral-storage  0 (0%)          0 (0%)
  hugepages-1Gi      0 (0%)          0 (0%)
  hugepages-2Mi      0 (0%)          0 (0%)
Events:              <none>
..


# check autoscaling
$ kubectl describe hpa.v2beta2.autoscaling php-apache
...
Metrics:              ( current / target )
  resource cpu on pods  (as a percentage of request):  0% (1m) / 50%


# get more details of autoscaling config by using -o -yaml
$ kubectl get hpa.v2beta2.autoscaling php-apache -o yaml
...
spec:
  maxReplicas: 10
  metrics:
  - resource:
      name: cpu
      target:
        averageUtilization: 50  <-- use avg metrics
        type: Utilization
```

4.2   Cluster Autoscaler (CA) - Nodes level auto-scaling

This feature can automatically adjusts the size of a Kubernetes Cluster so that all pods have a place to run and there are no unneeded nodes.

It is trigger by one of the following conditions:

- There are pods that failed to run in the cluster due to insufficient resources.
  It checks to see whether there are any pending pods and increases the size of the cluster so that these pods can be created.

- There are nodes in the cluster that have been underutilized for an extended period of time and their pods can be placed on other existing nodes.
  In this case, the CA deallocates idle nodes to keep the cluster at the optimal size.

Currently it is mainly provided by cloud providers e.g: GCP, AWS, Azure etc. Please see more details at:
https://github.com/kubernetes/autoscaler/tree/master/cluster-autoscaler

For our home network, we normally need to manually add/delete nodes.

4.2.1   Overprovisioning

Overprovisioning can be configured using deployment running pause pods with very low assigned priority which keeps resources that can be used by other pods.

It works as the following: **If there is not enough resources then pause pods are preempted and new pods take their place. Next pause pods become unschedulable and force CA to scale up the cluster.**

```
$ cat op.yaml
apiVersion: scheduling.k8s.io/v1beta1
kind: PriorityClass
metadata:
  name: overprovisioning
value: -1                                    <-- this is the key, low priority
globalDefault: false
description: "Priority class used by overprovisioning."
---
apiVersion: apps/v1
kind: Deployment
metadata:
  name: overprovisioning
```

```
  namespace: kube-system
spec:
  replicas: 1
  selector:
    matchLabels:
      run: overprovisioning
  template:
    metadata:
      labels:
        run: overprovisioning
    spec:
      priorityClassName: overprovisioning
      containers:
      - name: reserve-resources
        image: k8s.gcr.io/pause          <-- a pause container
        resources:
          requests:
            cpu: 300m
            memory: 500Mi

$ kubectl apply -f op.yaml

$ kubectl get pods -n kube-system
NAME                               READY    STATUS    RESTARTS    AGE
overprovisioning-5b965786d4-t5ldg  1/1      Running   0           33s
```

More details can be found at:

https://github.com/kubernetes/autoscaler/blob/master/cluster-autoscaler/FAQ.md

Chapter 5

Storage

There are many similar, yet confusing terms existed in both K8s and docker, thus make it hard for us to grasp it quickly. In this chapter, I will try to explain the most-often-used terms in K8s.

Tip

Please forget all docker's storage terms at least for this book.

5.1   volumes, volumeMounts

A volume in K8s has an explicit lifetime - the same lifetime as the Pod. That means a volume will outlive any containers inside a Pod, and data is preserved across Container restarts. But will cease to exist once Pod is gone.

Normally we claim/define a volume at pod level, then use volumeMounts to mount the volume inside a container.

A concrete example is :

```
# a typical volume and how to mount it
...
spec:
  volumes:                            <-- claim a volume
  - name: cache-volume                <-- the name of this volume
    emptyDir: {}                      <-- emptyDir type volume
```

```
  initContainers:
 - name: init-healthy
   image: busybox:1.28
   volumeMounts:                        <-- mount a volume inside container
    - name: cache-volume                <-- which volume we want to mount
     mountPath: /cache                  <-- mount it as /cache
   command: ['sh','-c', " touch /cache/healthy"]
...
```

Some useful volume type are:

- emptyDir : It is created when a Pod is assigned to a Node, initially is empty. It is good to store transient data etc.

- hostPath : It mounts a file or directory from the host/node's filesystem into a Pod.

- nfs: mount an external NFS share to a pod.

- persistentVolumeClaim: It is used to mount a PersistentVolume into a Pod. This is a quite useful volume type especially in the cloud environment. We will see it later for more details.

- many other types are documented at:
  https://kubernetes.io/docs/concepts/storage/volumes

5.2   PersistentVolume and PersistentVolumeClaim

A **PersistentVolume (PV)** is a piece of storage in the cluster that has been provisioned by an administrator (statically) or dynamically provisioned using Storage Classes. It is a cluster resource. Its life-cycle is independent of any individual Pod that uses the PV.

A pod can request a PV using **PersistentVolumeClaim (PVC)**.

In many cases, we prefer to use storage classes as it is dynamic and more flexible. It allows storage volumes to be created on-demand.

5.3   Storage Classes

Each StorageClass contains the fields provisioner, parameters, and reclaimPolicy, It is used when a PersistentVolume belonging to the class needs to be dynamically provisioned.

The **provisioner**, determines what kind of volume plugin will be used for provisioning PVs. The plugin is the key component under the hook that will actually do the job for us.

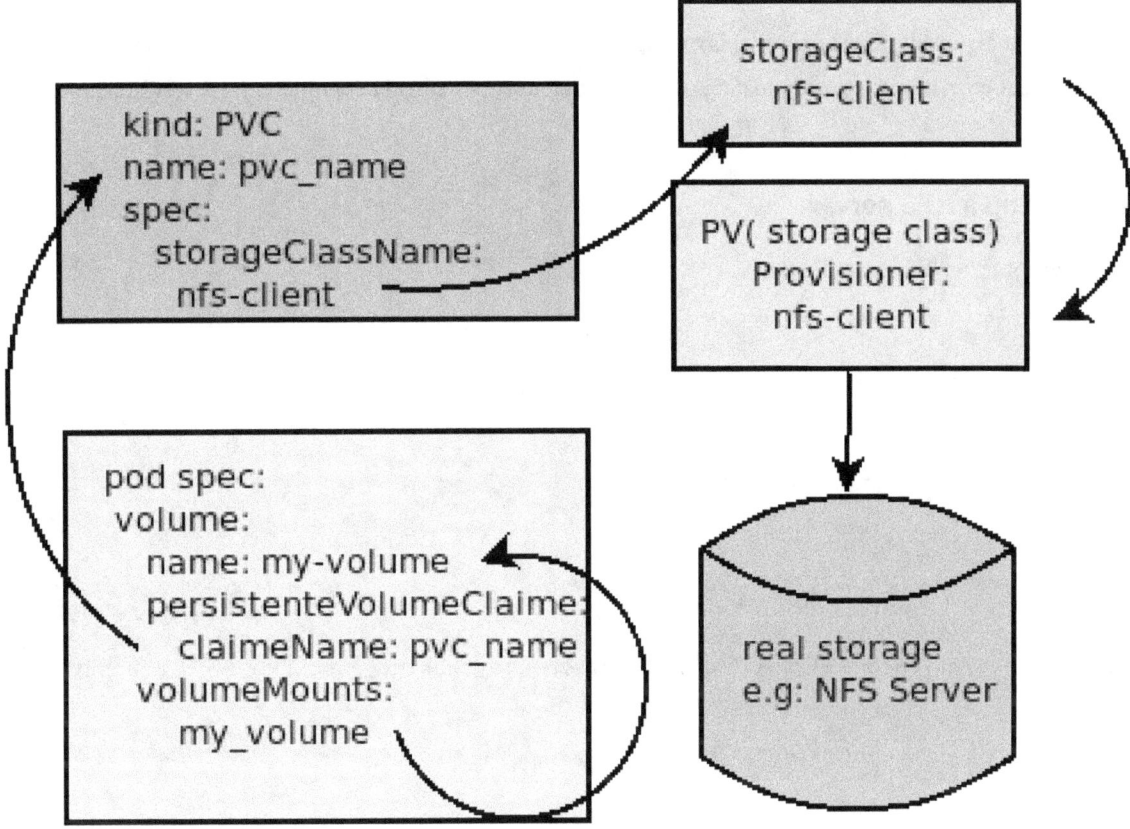

Figure 5.1: volume, pv/pvc,storage class and its provisioner relationship

The figure above showed the relationship between volume, pvc/pv, storage class, and its provisioner's relationship.

There are many build-in and external (third-party) plugins, see:

https://kubernetes.io/docs/concepts/storage/storage-classes/

https://github.com/kubernetes-retired/external-storage

5.4   NFS storage classes example

Let's see a concrete example.

We will use an nfs-client provisioner in this example.

The NFS client provisioner is an automatic provisioner that uses our already configured NFS server, automatically creating PV.

5.4.1   set up a NFS server

We need to set up a NFS server first.

```
# install nfs-server on debian-based server
# please adjust for your OS
$ apt-get install nfs-kernel-server

# for security reason
# let change our nfs share to nobody:nogroup
# chown -R nobody.nogroup /data/storage/k8s/nfs

# config export
# $ cat /etc/exports
# no_root_squash is needed as some k8s application
# need root access so that it can chmod/chown on this mounted volume
/data/storage/k8s/nfs 192.168.86.0/24(rw,sync,no_subtree_check,no_root_squash)

# export nfs share
# or you can : systemctl restart nfs-server
$ exportfs -rav

# testing from a nfs-client
# install nfs client
$ apt-get install nfs-common
$ mount -t nfs your_nfs_server_ip:/data/storage/k8s/nfs test

$ cd test
# we should be able to use nobody or root to touch a file
$ sudo -u nobody touch test.txt
# or use  sudo, as NFS root_squash will mapping root as nobody in NFS server
$ sudo touch test.txt
```

5.4.2   install nfs-client provisioner using helm

Helm have a nice nfs-client-provisioner chart to make our life easier.

https://github.com/kubernetes-sigs/nfs-subdir-external-provisioner

```
# helm repo add nfs-subdir-external-provisioner https://kubernetes-sigs.github.io ←
    /nfs-subdir-external-provisioner/
# install nfs-client provisioner
$ helm install nfs-subdir-external-provisioner nfs-subdir-external-provisioner/ ←
    nfs-subdir-external-provisioner \
      --set nfs.server=192.168.86.30  \
      --set nfs.path=/data/storage/k8s/nfs stable/nfs-client-provisioner

# check if we create storage class or not
$ kubectl get storageclass
NAME PROVISIONER          RECLAIMPOLICY    VOLUMEBINDINGMODE    ALLOWVOLUMEEXPANSION
nfs-client cluster.local
/nfs-client-provisioner
-1599319108              Delete           Immediate            true

# just look at the storage class yaml file
$ kubectl edit storageclass nfs-client
allowVolumeExpansion: true
apiVersion: storage.k8s.io/v1
kind: StorageClass                              <-- StorageClass
metadata:
  annotations:
    meta.helm.sh/release-name: nfs-client-provisioner-1599319108
    meta.helm.sh/release-namespace: default
  creationTimestamp: "2020-09-05T15:18:34Z"
  labels:
    app: nfs-client-provisioner
    app.kubernetes.io/managed-by: Helm
    chart: nfs-client-provisioner-1.2.9
    heritage: Helm
    release: nfs-client-provisioner-1599319108
  name: nfs-client                              <-- name of this storageclass
  resourceVersion: "2102535"
  selfLink: /apis/storage.k8s.io/v1/storageclasses/nfs-client
  uid: 31cbc132-b0d7-4974-aebc-d1d8d65cbccc
parameters:
  archiveOnDelete: "true"
```

```
provisioner: cluster.local/nfs-client-provisioner-1599319108 <-- provisioner pod
reclaimPolicy: Delete
volumeBindingMode: Immediate


# check nfs-client provisioner running or not
$ kubectl get pods -o wide | grep nfs
NAME                             READY STATUS RESTARTS AGE        IP            NODE
nfs-client-provisioner
1599319108-7978f6d6c-qnfkf 1/1  Running 0         58m       10.36.0.8     openstack01
```

Tip

If that pod is stuck at ContainerCreating, check "kubectl describe node nfs-client-provisioner-1599319108-7978f6d6c-qnfkf", one problem I had was there was no nfs-common (nfs-client) installed on that node openstack01. Once installed, it went smoothly.

5.4.3   create a pvc using the storage class

Let's create a PVC/PV that a pod can use later.

```
# pvc1.yaml
kind: PersistentVolumeClaim                 <-- PVC
apiVersion: v1
metadata:
  name: pvc1
  annotations:
    volume.beta.kubernetes.io/storage-class: nfs-client
spec:
  storageClassName: nfs-client              <-- use this storage class
  accessModes:
    - ReadWriteMany                         <-- we can read/write it
  resources:
    requests:
      storage: 50Mi                         <-- requested storage size 50M

$ kubectl apply -f ./pvc1.yaml
persistentvolumeclaim/pvc1 created

$ kubectl get pvc
```

```
NAME    STATUS    VOLUME     CAPACITY    ACCESS MODES    STORAGECLASS   AGE
pvc1    Pending                                          nfs-client     35s

# check PVC
$ kubectl get pvc
NAME    STATUS    VOLUME                  CAPACITY   ACCESS MODES    STORAGECLASS   AGE
pvc1    Bound     pvc-bbe523e3-9ab9-49b5
                  -bb08-20cce1db33b0      50Mi       RWX             nfs-client     51m


# Now check if a PV was created by this PVC
$ kubectl get pv
NAME        CAPACITY   ACCESS    RECLAIM    STATUS   CLAIM    STORAGECLASS REASON    AGE
pvc-bbe52..            MODES     POLICY
            50Mi       RWX       Delete     Bound    default nfs-client              21m
                                                     /pvc1
```

5.4.4   create a pod to use that pvc

```
$ more test-pvc-pod.yaml
apiVersion: v1
kind: Pod
metadata:
  name: busybox
spec:
  volumes:
  - name: nfs-volume                    <-- name of this volume
    persistentVolumeClaim:              <-- our volume type: PVC
      claimName: pvc1                    <-- previous pvc name
  containers:
  - image: busybox
    name: busybox
    command: ["/bin/sh"]
    args: ["-c", "sleep 600"]
    volumeMounts:                       <-- mount our volume
    - name: nfs-volume                  <-- name of pv volume defined
      mountPath: /pvc1_data             <-- mounting path inside container
```

Let's start the pod:

```
$ kubectl apply -f test-pvc-pod.yaml

# let's go inside that pod
$ kubectl exec -it busybox -- ./bin/sh

# go to the nfs share
$ cd /pvc1_data/

# make some changes
$ mkdir test && cd test && touch test/test.txt
$ /pvc1_data/test # ls -la
total 8
drwxr-xr-x    2 root     root          4096 Sep  5 20:07 .
drwxrwxrwx    3 root     root          4096 Sep  5 20:07 ..
-rw-r--r--    1 root     root             0 Sep  5 20:07 test.txt
```

Let's check the external nfs server:

```
cd /data/storage/k8s/nfs
$ find default-pvc1-pvc-bbe523e3-9ab9-49b5-bb08-20cce1db33b0/
default-pvc1-pvc-bbe523e3-9ab9-49b5-bb08-20cce1db33b0/
default-pvc1-pvc-bbe523e3-9ab9-49b5-bb08-20cce1db33b0/test
default-pvc1-pvc-bbe523e3-9ab9-49b5-bb08-20cce1db33b0/test/test.txt
```

We verify that the file actually has been created successfully.

Tip
If you PVC, kubectl delete pvc pvc1, this dir become:
archived-default-pvc1-pvc-bbe523e3-9ab9-49b5-bb08-20cce1db33b0

Chapter 6

Stateful Applications

What is a stateful application?

What is a stateless application?

They are probably loosely defined in the online documents, thus bring some confusion.

Based on my understanding and documents online, such as:
https://kubernetes.io/docs/tutorials/stateful-application/
https://cloud.google.com/kubernetes-engine/docs/how-to/stateful-apps ,

In the context of K8s:

- A **stateless application** has no persistent storage or volume associated with it.

- A **stateful application** saves data to persistent disk storage for use by the server, by clients, and by other applications.

We should NOT confuse Stateful application with StatefulSets.

Not all stateful applications need to use StatefulSets.

6.1   Deploy a stateful app using Deployment

Actually some stateful applications can be deployed using Deployment/Replicate with persistent storage.

A good example is:

https://kubernetes.io/docs/tutorials/stateful-application/mysql-wordpress-persistent-volume/

, where it uses Deployment with PV for a typical stateful application: WordPress and Mysql.

I will skip the content as it is easy to understand.

Please refer to the previous K8s url for more details.

6.2 Deploy a stateful application using StatefulSet (cassandra)

On the other hand, many stateful applications are well suited to take advantage of the features that StatefulSets can offer. Here, for a demo purpose, we will deploy a stateful application using StatefulSets.

Apache Cassandra is a free and open-source, distributed, wide column store, NoSQL database management system designed to handle large amounts of data across many commodity servers, providing high availability with no single point of failure.

I mainly followed the instruction from:

https://kubernetes.io/docs/tutorials/stateful-application/cassandra/

6.2.1 Create a Headless Service

In many cases, a pod inside a statefulset needs a way to discover all other pods' ip addresses in a predictable fashion.

In this case, we don't need load-balancing and a single Service IP, but we just need a way to find all pods's ip for our cassandra cluster.

A headless service is perfect for this. We can create a **headless service** by explicitly specifying "None" for the cluster IP (.spec.clusterIP).

Here, we create a headless service, cassandra, to publish the IP addresses of Pods in the StatefulSet, cassandra.

Tip

You don't have to use a Headless Service for a StatefulSet, but it often makes sense to use one if you want to take advantage of the sticky identity of each Pod in a StatefulService etc.

For headless Services, a cluster IP is not allocated, kube-proxy does not handle these Services, and there is no load balancing or proxying done by the platform for them. But DNS for this service is automatically configured to be used within the K8s cluster. You will see it in more detail later.

```
# create headless service
# $ cat cassandra-service.yaml
apiVersion: v1
kind: Service
metadata:
  labels:
    app: cassandra
  name: cassandra
spec:
  clusterIP: None          <-- headless service
  ports:
  - port: 9042
  selector:
    app: cassandra

$ kubectl apply -f cassandra-service.yaml

# check
$ kubectl get svc
NAME         TYPE         CLUSTER-IP     EXTERNAL-IP    PORT(S)     AGE
cassandra    ClusterIP    None           <none>         9042/TCP    88m

# at this time Endpoints are empty
$ kubectl describe svc cassandra
Name:               cassandra
Namespace:          default
Labels:             app=cassandra
Annotations:        <none>
Selector:           app=cassandra
Type:               ClusterIP
IP:                 None
Port:               <unset>   9042/TCP
TargetPort:         9042/TCP
Endpoints:
Session Affinity:   None
Events:             <none>
```

6.2.2   Create cassandra StatefulSets pod

The next step is to really create a stateful resource.

The statefulset definition for cassandra can be downloaded at:

https://k8s.io/examples/application/cassandra/cassandra-statefulset.yaml

Since we have our own nfs-client storage class in this cluster, we need to modify yaml a little bit.

The parameters for StatefulSet are quite similar to Deployment.

```
$ wget //k8s.io/examples/application/cassandra/cassandra-statefulset.yaml

# remove storage class and modify the storage class within
# the statefulset accordingly

$ cat cassandra-statefulset.yaml
apiVersion: apps/v1
kind: StatefulSet                         <-- statefulSet, similar to Deployment
metadata:
  name: cassandra                         <--used for hostname/podname-0/1/2 etc.
  labels:
    app: cassandra
spec:
  serviceName: cassandra
  replicas: 3                             <-- stateful replica
  selector:
    matchLabels:
      app: cassandra
  template:
    metadata:
      labels:
        app: cassandra
    spec:
      terminationGracePeriodSeconds: 1800
      containers:
      - name: cassandra
        image: gcr.io/google-samples/cassandra:v13
        imagePullPolicy: Always
        ports:
        - containerPort: 7000
          name: intra-node
        - containerPort: 7001
          name: tls-intra-node
        - containerPort: 7199
          name: jmx
        - containerPort: 9042
          name: cql
```

```
            resources:
              limits:
                cpu: "500m"
                memory: "1Gi"
              requests:
                cpu: "500m"
                memory: "1Gi"
            securityContext:
              capabilities:
                add:
                  - IPC_LOCK
            lifecycle:
              preStop:
                exec:
                  command:
                  - /bin/sh
                  - -c
                  - nodetool drain
            env:
              - name: MAX_HEAP_SIZE
                value: 512M
              - name: HEAP_NEWSIZE
                value: 100M
              - name: CASSANDRA_SEEDS
                value: "cassandra-0.cassandra.default.svc.cluster.local"
              - name: CASSANDRA_CLUSTER_NAME
                value: "K8Demo"
              - name: CASSANDRA_DC
                value: "DC1-K8Demo"
              - name: CASSANDRA_RACK
                value: "Rack1-K8Demo"
              - name: POD_IP
                valueFrom:
                  fieldRef:
                    fieldPath: status.podIP
            readinessProbe:
              exec:
                command:
                - /bin/bash
                - -c
                - /ready-probe.sh
              initialDelaySeconds: 15
```

```
        timeoutSeconds: 5
        # These volume mounts are persistent. They are like inline claims,
        # but not exactly because the names need to match exactly one of
        # the stateful pod volumes.
        volumeMounts:
        - name: cassandra-data
          mountPath: /cassandra_data
  # These are converted to volume claims by the controller
  # and mounted at the paths mentioned above.
  # do not use these in production until ssd GCEPersistentDisk or other ssd pd
  volumeClaimTemplates:                           <-- volume template instead of pvc
  - metadata:
      name: cassandra-data
    spec:
      accessModes: [ "ReadWriteOnce" ]
      storageClassName: nfs-client                <-- here is our storage class
      resources:
        requests:
          storage: 1Gi

# create statefulset resource
$ kubectl apply -f ./cassandra-statefulset.yaml
```

6.2.3 Ordered pod create and stable network identities

For a StatefulSet with n replicas, when Pods are being deployed, they are created sequentially, ordered from {0..n-1}. The Pods' names take the form <statefulset name>-<ordinal index>, and each pod's hostname also be named similarly. That is called **ordered pod creation**.

In this case, we will get pods named: cassandra-0, cassandra-1 ... etc.

```
# k8s will start statefulset pod one by one!
$ kubectl get pods
NAME              READY     STATUS              RESTARTS    AGE
cassandra-0       0/1       ContainerCreating   0           7s

# after a while, all 3 pods should be up
$  kubectl get pods -o wide
NAME          READY     STATUS    RESTARTS   AGE     IP            NODE
cassandra-0   1/1       Running   0          16m     10.36.0.10    openstack01
cassandra-1   1/1       Running   0          14m     10.32.0.6     mailsrv
```

```
cassandra-2 0/1     Running     0           55s     10.32.0.7     mailsrv

# now check cassandra status
$ kubectl exec -it cassandra-0 -- nodetool status
Datacenter: DC1-K8Demo
=======================
Status=Up/Down
|/ State=Normal/Leaving/Joining/Moving
--  Address     Load        Tokens  Owns (effective)  Host ID       Rack
UN  10.32.0.6   103.82 KiB  32      65.5%             81447f17-..   Rack1-K8Demo
UN  10.32.0.7   152.29 KiB  32      71.2%             9a9f1e24-..   Rack1-K8Demo
UN  10.36.0.10  104.54 KiB  32      63.3%             8ea1d427-..   Rack1-K8Demo

# now headless service endpoint is filled with pods' ip
$ kubectl describe svc cassandra
Name:             cassandra
Namespace:        default
Labels:           app=cassandra
Annotations:      <none>
Selector:         app=cassandra
Type:             ClusterIP
IP:               None
Port:             <unset>  9042/TCP
TargetPort:       9042/TCP
Endpoints:        10.32.0.6:9042,10.36.0.10:9042,10.36.0.7:9042
Session Affinity: None
Events:           <none>
```

If we delete one of the pod, the StatefulSets will re-created a new pod with a new ip, but exact same hostname, SRV?A records etc.

Thus it is important NOT to configure other applications to connect to Pods in a StatefulSet by IP address.

Instead, if we need to find and connect to the active members of a StatefulSet, we should query the CNAME of the headless Service (e.g.: cassandra.default.svc.cluster.local). The SRV records associated with the CNAME will contain only the Pods in the StatefulSet that are Running and Ready.

Let's check it:

```
# login to one of cassandra pod
$ kubectl exec -it cassandra-0 -- /bin/bash

# install nslookup etc
```

```
$ apt-get update && apt-get install dnsutils

$ hostname
cassandra-0

root@cassandra-0:/# nslookup cassandra-0.cassandra
Server:         10.96.0.10
Address:        10.96.0.10#53

Name:   cassandra-0.cassandra.default.svc.cluster.local
Address: 10.36.0.10

root@cassandra-0:/# nslookup cassandra.default.svc.cluster.local
Server:         10.96.0.10
Address:        10.96.0.10#53

Name:   cassandra.default.svc.cluster.local
Address: 10.32.0.6
Name:   cassandra.default.svc.cluster.local
Address: 10.36.0.7
Name:   cassandra.default.svc.cluster.local
Address: 10.36.0.10
```

6.2.4 Stable storage

The **volumeClaimTemplates** in that yaml file will instruct K8s to provide a stable storage pod by creating a
PersistentVolumes for each pod, which is actually provisioned by a PersistentVolume Provisioner. The parameters
for volumeClaimTemplates are similar to PVC.

In this case, we use nfs-client as the storageClassName.

```
# now check  pvc
$ kubectl get pvc -l app=cassandra
NAME                        STATUS VOLUME CAPACITY ACCESS STORAGECLASS  AGE
cassandra-data-cassandra-0 Bound  pvc-e.. 1Gi      RWO    nfs-client    9m30s
cassandra-data-cassandra-1 Bound  pvc-v.. 1Gi      RWO    nfs-client    8m
cassandra-data-cassandra-2 Bound  pvc-8.. 1Gi      RWO    nfs-client    6m1s

# now on NFS server, check
$ /data/storage/k8s/nfs# ls -la default-cassandra-data-cassandra-0..
total 24
```

```
drwx------   6 minge   root     4096 Sep  6 16:19 .
drwxr-xr-x 16 nobody  nogroup 4096 Sep  6 16:22 ..
drwxr-xr-x  2 minge   minge    4096 Sep  6 16:19 commitlog
drwxr-xr-x  7 minge   minge    4096 Sep  6 16:20 data
drwxr-xr-x  2 minge   minge    4096 Sep  6 16:19 hints
drwxr-xr-x  2 minge   minge    4096 Sep  6 16:19 saved_caches
```

6.2.5   Access cassandra headless service from K8s node (inside K8s cluster)

On any of the nodes inside the K8s cluster, we can access the service by looking-up the service DNS, then use one of the ip addresses to access its service at tcp port: 9042.

```
# on any of node in K8s cluster, we can try:

$ nslookup cassandra.default.svc.cluster.local 10.96.0.10
...
Name:    cassandra.default.svc.cluster.local
Address: 10.32.0.6
Name:    cassandra.default.svc.cluster.local
Address: 10.36.0.9

# need to install cqlsh  on this node
$ pip install cqlsh

# try on client
export CQLSH_HOST="10.36.0.6"
cqlsh --cqlversion=3.4.4

cqlsh>
```

6.2.6   Access cassandra headless service from outside

Well, login to node , then access the service is not convenient at all.

Remember a headless service just exposes a DNS service that can be accessed only internally within the K8s cluster, its main purpose is for internal usage.

Thus, we need to install a LoadBalancer so that we can access it from outside.

```
$ cat cassandra_external.xml
apiVersion: v1
kind: Service
metadata:
  labels:
    app: cassandra
  name: cassandra-ext
spec:
  type: LoadBalancer
  ports:
    - port: 9042
  selector:
    app: cassandra

$ kubectl apply -f ./cassandra_external.xml

$ kubectl get svc
NAME            TYPE          CLUSTER-IP      EXTERNAL-IP      PORT(S)          AGE
cassandra       ClusterIP     None            <none>           9042/TCP         23h
cassandra-ext   LoadBalancer  10.100.81.181   192.168.86.82    9042:32601/TCP   5s
```

Now we should be able to access the service at: 192.168.86.82:9042

Tip

If we want to access it using DNS, we need to add 192.168.86.82 to our external DNS (not K8s DNS).

6.2.7 Cassandra quick start

I followed this: https://www.datastax.com/blog/2012/01/getting-started-apache-cassandra

On any host outside the cluster,

```
# on host not inside the K8s cluster
# install cqlsh
$ pip install cqlsh

# try on client
#export CQLSH_HOST="10.36.0.10"
export CQLSH_HOST="192.168.86.82"
```

```
cqlsh --cqlversion=3.4.4

# keyspace is similar to a database in a relational db.
cqlsh> create keyspace dev with replication =
                      {'class':'SimpleStrategy','replication_factor':1};
cqlsh> use dev;

# create a table
cqlsh:dev> create table emp (empid int primary key,emp_first varchar, \
                          emp_last varchar, emp_dept varchar);

# insert a db
cqlsh:dev> insert into emp (empid, emp_first, emp_last, emp_dept)
                          values (1,'fred','smith','eng');

# select
cqlsh:dev> select * from emp;
 empid | emp_dept | emp_first | emp_last
-------+----------+-----------+----------
     1 |      eng |      fred |    smith
(1 rows)

# update
cqlsh:dev> update emp set emp_dept = 'fin' where empid = 1;

cqlsh:dev> select * from emp;
 empid | emp_dept | emp_first | emp_last
-------+----------+-----------+----------
     1 |      fin |      fred |    smith
(1 rows)

# create secondary index
cqlsh:dev> create index idx_dept on emp(emp_dept);
cqlsh:dev> select * from emp where emp_dept = 'fin';
 empid | emp_dept | emp_first | emp_last
-------+----------+-----------+----------
     1 |      fin |      fred |    smith
```

6.2.8 Scaling a StatefulSet

we can simply scale up/down StatefulSet by change the replica in the yaml file or doing it in the command line:

```
# scale up
kubectl scale sts cassandra --replicas=5
# scale down
kubectl scale sts cassandra --replicas=2
```

Remember, StatefulSet will do **Ordered Pod Termination**, which means the K8s will delete one Pod at a time, in reverse order with respect to its ordinal index, and will wait for each to be completely shutdown before deleting the next.

The PersistentVolumeClaims and PersistentVolumes will not be deleted while scaling down. Actually, they (and the headless service) will not be deleted even we delete the StatefulSet, we need to manually or write a script to clean it up. The reason is: the data are generally very useful/valuable even those stateful applications are shutdown/offline.

6.2.9 Clean up a StatefulSet

As shown in previous section, for a cleanup, we need to delete statefulset, pvc/pv, and headless service etc resources.

The following showed how to to delete everything in the Cassandra StatefulSet:

```
grace=$(kubectl get pod cassandra-0 \
  -o=jsonpath='{.spec.terminationGracePeriodSeconds}') \
  && kubectl delete statefulset -l app=cassandra \
  && echo "Sleeping ${grace} seconds" 1>&2 \
  && sleep $grace \
  && kubectl delete persistentvolumeclaim -l app=cassandra
Run the following command to delete the Service you set up for Cassandra:

kubectl delete service -l app=cassandra

cassandra-0
 kubectl --v=8 logs cassandra-0
chown: changing ownership of '/cassandra_data': Operation not permitted
```

Chapter 7

Role-Based Access Control (RBAC)

RBAC is a popular authorization plugins for K8s, but somehow looks daunting to understand.

Tip
K8s also includes other authorization plugins, such as the Attribute-based access control (ABAC) plugin, a Web-Hook plugin and custom plugin implementations.

To understand RBAC, we first need to understand the following key concepts:

- **Identity**: K8s has two kinds of identities.

  - **Service accounts** are created and managed by K8s and are generally associated with components running inside the cluster.
  - **((User accounts)** are generally associated with actual users of the cluster etc.

- A **Role** or **ClusterRole** contains rules that represent a set of permissions. Permissions are purely additive (there are no "deny" rules). A Role always sets permissions within a particular namespace; while ClusterRole is a non-namespaced resource.
  For example, the app_dev role might represent the ability to create Pods and services.

- A **RoleBinding** grants the permissions defined in a role to a user or set of users. A RoleBinding grants permissions within a specific namespace whereas a **ClusterRoleBinding** grants that access cluster-wide.

In short, the RBAC procedure is:

- First, create a service account or a normal user account.

- then create a role, or cluster role.

- finally, we create a rolebinding or clusterrolebiding to grant permission/role to our account/identities.

For example, binding the app_dev role to the user identity alice indicates that Alice has the ability to create Pods and services.

7.1 context vs namespace

A context in K8s is a group of access parameters. Each context contains a cluster, a user, and a namespace. Each of the contexts that have been used will be available on your .kubeconfig.

```
$ kubectl config current-context
kubernetes-admin@kubernetes

$ kubectl config get-clusters
NAME
kubernetes
$ kubectl config get-contexts
CURRENT   NAME                           CLUSTER      AUTHINFO            NAMESPACE
          employee-context              kubernetes   employee            office
*         kubernetes-admin@kubernetes   kubernetes   kubernetes-admin
```

A Namespace is a logical partition inside a specific cluster to manage resources and constraints.

```
$ kubectl get namespace
NAME                   STATUS   AGE
default                Active   12d
ingress-controller     Active   9d
kube-node-lease        Active   12d
kube-public            Active   12d
kube-system            Active   12d
kube-verify            Active   11d
kubernetes-dashboard   Active   11d
metallb-system         Active   11d
office                 Active   74m
```

7.2   create a service account, role and rolebinding

In the previous chapter where we install DashboardUI, We showed how to create a service account and how to bind a service account with a cluster-admin role.

7.3   create a normal user account, role and rolebinding

According to K8s document:

Kubernetes does not have objects which represent normal user accounts. Normal users cannot be added to a cluster through an API call.

Even though normal user cannot be added via an API call, but any user that presents a valid certificate signed by the cluster's certificate authority (CA) is considered authenticated. In this configuration, Kubernetes determines the username from the common name field in the *subject* of the cert (e.g., "/CN=bob"). From there, the role based access control (RBAC) sub-system would determine whether the user is authorized to perform a specific operation on a resource.

Thus, normal users are assumed to be managed by an outside, independent service. Here we will show a way to add a normal user.

I mainly followed:

https://docs.bitnami.com/tutorials/configure-rbac-in-your-kubernetes-cluster/

https://www.adaltas.com/en/2019/08/07/users-rbac-kubernetes/

The following showed how to create/add a normal user in k8s.

7.3.1   Create a new namespace and user credentials

```
# assume we are on linux/unix box
# let's create a user first
$ useradd employee && cd /home/employee

# create namespace
$ kubectl create namespace office

# generate a private key for this user
$ openssl genrsa -out employee.key 2048
```

```
# create certificate sign request
$ openssl req -new -key employee.key -out employee.csr \
           -subj "/CN=employee/O=comrite"

$ export CA_LOCATION="/etc/kubernetes/pki/"

# generate final certificate using K8s's CA
$ sudo openssl x509 -req -in employee.csr -CA $CA_LOCATION/ca.crt \
   -CAkey $CA_LOCATION/ca.key -CAcreateserial -out employee.crt -days 500
Signature ok
subject=CN = employee, O = comrite
Getting CA Private Key

# Sets a user entry in kubeconfig
$ kubectl config set-credentials employee \
  --client-certificate=/your_dir/employee.crt \
   --client-key=/your/employee.key
User "employee" set.

# Sets a new context entry in kubeconfig
$ kubectl config set-context employee-context
--cluster=kubernetes --namespace=office --user=employee

# check our kubeconfig
$ kubectl config view
apiVersion: v1
clusters:
- cluster:
    certificate-authority-data: DATA+OMITTED
    server: https://192.168.86.30:6443
  name: kubernetes
contexts:
- context:
    cluster: kubernetes
    namespace: office
    user: employee
  name: employee-context
- context:
    cluster: kubernetes
    user: kubernetes-admin
  name: kubernetes-admin@kubernetes
```

```
current-context: kubernetes-admin@kubernetes
kind: Config
preferences: {}
users:
- name: employee
  user:
    client-certificate: /home/mwang/Development/dev-ops/k8s-hpa/rbac/employee.crt
    client-key: /home/mwang/Development/dev-ops/k8s-hpa/rbac/employee.key
- name: kubernetes-admin
  user:
    client-certificate-data: REDACTED
    client-key-data: REDACTED

# show our current-context
$ kubectl config current-context
kubernetes-admin@kubernetes
```

7.3.2   Create the role and rolebinding

```
# use employee-context to get pods,
# it will failed as we do not set role and rolebinding yet
$ kubectl --context=employee-context get pods
Error from server (Forbidden): pods is forbidden: User "employee"
cannot list resource "pods" in API group "" in the namespace "office"

# we need to create a role
$ cat role-deployment-manager.yaml
kind: Role
apiVersion: rbac.authorization.k8s.io/v1beta1
metadata:
  namespace: office
  name: deployment-manager
rules:
- apiGroups: ["", "extensions", "apps"]
  resources: ["deployments", "replicasets", "pods"]
  verbs: ["get", "list", "watch", "create", "update", "patch", "delete"]

# create a role
$ kubectl create -f role-deployment-manager.yaml
```

```
$ kubectl get roles -n office
NAME                 CREATED AT
deployment-manager   2020-09-08T02:29:56Z


# create a role binding
# binding user employee to the previous role
$ cat rolebinding-deployment-manager.yaml
kind: RoleBinding
apiVersion: rbac.authorization.k8s.io/v1beta1
metadata:
  name: deployment-manager-binding
  namespace: office
subjects:
- kind: User
  name: employee
  apiGroup: ""
roleRef:
  kind: Role
  name: deployment-manager
  apiGroup: ""

$ kubectl create -f rolebinding-deployment-manager.yaml
$ kubectl get rolebinding -n office
NAME                         ROLE                      AGE
deployment-manager-binding   Role/deployment-manager   34m
```

7.3.3 Testing the normal user using context

```
# now we can test it
$ kubectl --context=employee-context run --image bitnami/dokuwiki mydokuwiki
pod/mydokuwiki created

# check it
$ kubectl --context=employee-context get pods
NAME                        READY   STATUS    RESTARTS   AGE
mydokuwiki                  1/1     Running   0          106s
php-apache-d4cf67d68-rfj6b  1/1     Running   0          2m41s
```

```
# use this role for other namespace
# will fail as it is not permitted in the role
$ kubectl --context=employee-context get pods --namespace=default
Error from server (Forbidden): pods is forbidden: User "employee"
cannot list resource "pods" in API group "" in the namespace "default"
```

Chapter 8

Misc

Here are some additional items worth being mentioned here.

8.1 Job

A **Job** creates one or more Pods. It is useful for things we only want to do once.

Let's just look at an example:

```
$ cat pi.yaml
apiVersion: batch/v1
kind: Job                                      <-- job
metadata:
  name: pi
spec:
  template:
    spec:
      containers:
      - name: pi
        image: perl
        command: ["perl", "-Mbignum=bpi", "-wle", "print bpi(2000)"]
      restartPolicy: Never
  backoffLimit: 4
```

```
# create job
$ kubectl apply -f ./pi.yaml

# check
$ kubectl get jobs
NAME    COMPLETIONS    DURATION    AGE
pi      0/1            4s          4s

$ kubectl describe job pi
Name:           pi
Namespace:      default
Selector:       controller-uid=5b5d83ce-fdfa-4cf4-b382-44b483effd39
Labels:         controller-uid=5b5d83ce-fdfa-4cf4-b382-44b483effd39
                job-name=pi
Annotations:    <none>
Parallelism:    1
Completions:    1
Start Time:     Mon, 07 Sep 2020 16:43:42 -0400
Pods Statuses:  1 Running / 0 Succeeded / 0 Failed
Pod Template:
  Labels:  controller-uid=5b5d83ce-fdfa-4cf4-b382-44b483effd39
           job-name=pi
  Containers:
   pi:
    Image:      perl
    Port:       <none>
    Host Port:  <none>
    Command:
      perl
      -Mbignum=bpi
      -wle
      print bpi(2000)
    Environment:  <none>
    Mounts:       <none>
  Volumes:        <none>
Events:
  Type    Reason          Age   From            Message
  ----    ------          ----  ----            -------
  Normal  SuccessfulCreate 10s  job-controller  Created pod: pi-x2jdn

$ kubectl get pods
NAME                                           READY   STATUS   RESTARTS   ↩
```

```
    AGE
pi-x2jdn                                              1/1     Running   0              ↩
    14s


# check result
$ kubectl logs pi-x2jdn
3.1415926535897932384626433832795028841971693937...
```

Normally we need to manually delete jobs.

```
# delete job, it will delete associated pod as well
$ kubectl delete job pi
```

You can read more details at:

https://kubernetes.io/docs/concepts/workloads/controllers/job/

8.2 CronJob

K8s also support **cronjobs,** which are useful for creating periodic and recurring tasks, like running backups or sending emails, They can also schedule individual tasks for a specific time, such as scheduling a Job for when your cluster is likely to be idle.

```
apiVersion: batch/v1beta1
kind: CronJob                      <-- cron job
metadata:
  name: hello
spec:
  schedule: "*/1 * * * *"          <-- schedule timing
  jobTemplate:
    spec:
      template:
        spec:
          containers:
          - name: hello
            image: busybox
            args:
```

```
        - /bin/sh
        - -c
        - date; echo Hello from the Kubernetes cluster
      restartPolicy: OnFailure
```

You can read more details at:

https://kubernetes.io/docs/concepts/workloads/controllers/cron-jobs/

8.3 ConfigMap

ConfigMap allows us to decouple configuration artifacts from image content to keep containerized applications portable. It is combined with the Pod right before it is run.

8.3.1 Create ConfigMap

We can create it from a file, directory, literal values.

```
# kubectl create configmap <map-name> <data-source>

# create it from literal for simplicity
$ kubectl create configmap special-config --from-literal=special.how=very \
  --from-literal=special.type=charm

# from file
# kubectl create configmap config-2 --from-file=my_conf/config.properties
# from dir
# kubectl create configmap config-3 --from-file=my_conf/configmap/

# check it
$ kubectl get configmap
NAME             DATA    AGE
special-config   2       5s

# view the config map
$ kubectl describe configmap configmap
Name:         special-config
Namespace:    default
```

```
Labels:         <none>
Annotations:    <none>

Data
====
special.how:
  --
very

special.type:
  --
charm
Events:    <none>
```

8.3.2   Using ConfigMap

ConfigMap can be used as:

(1) FileSystem, essentially we can mount configMap into a container.

```
$ cat fs.yaml
apiVersion: v1
kind: Pod
metadata:
  name: cm-test-pod
spec:
  containers:
    - name: test-container
      image: k8s.gcr.io/busybox
      command: [ "/bin/sh", "-c", "sleep 600" ]
      volumeMounts:
      - name: config-volume
        mountPath: /config
  volumes:
    - name: config-volume
      configMap:                     <-- use configMap as file system
        name: special-config
  restartPolicy: Never

# start pod
$ kubectl apply -f fs.yaml
```

```
pod/cm-test-pod created

$ kubectl get pod
NAME                                                        READY    STATUS     RESTARTS    ↩
   AGE
cm-test-pod                                                 1/1      Running    0           ↩
   10s

$ kubectl exec -it  cm-test-pod -- /bin/sh
/ # ls config
special.how    special.type

# cat special.how
very
# cat special.type
charm
```

(2) Environment variables, we can pass configMap as Environment variables.

```
apiVersion: v1
kind: Pod
metadata:
  name: env-test-pod
spec:
  containers:
    - name: test-container
      image: k8s.gcr.io/busybox
      command: [ "/bin/sh", "-c", "env" ]
      env:
        # Define the environment variable
      - name: SPECIAL_LEVEL_KEY
        valueFrom:
          configMapKeyRef:
# The ConfigMap containing the value you want to assign to SPECIAL_LEVEL_KEY
            name: special-config
              # Specify the key associated with the value
            key: special.how
  restartPolicy: Never

# check if env passed
$ kubectl logs -f  env-test-pod | grep SPEC
SPECIAL_LEVEL_KEY=very
```

8.4 Secrets

Currently secret is similar to ConfigMap in terms of how it is defined and how it is used.

The difference are secrets are obfuscated with a Base64 encoding, there could be more differences in the future.

In short:

- Use secrets for things which are actually secret like API keys, credentials, etc.

- Use config map for not-secret configuration data

More details at:

https://kubernetes.io/docs/concepts/configuration/secret/

Chapter 9

Cheat Sheet

9.1   config related

```
# auto complete
source <(kubectl completion bash)

# use multiple kubeconfig files at the same time and view merged config
KUBECONFIG=~/.kube/config:~/.kube/kubconfig2

# Display addresses of the master and services
kubectl cluster-info

# config related
kubectl config view

# display list of contexts
kubectl config get-contexts

# display the current-context
kubectl config current-context

# set the default context to my-cluster-name
kubectl config use-context my-cluster-name
```

```
# set the default context to my-cluster-name
kubectl config set-context --current --namespace=office

# delete user foo
kubectl config unset users.foo
```

9.2   kubectl related

```
# Kubectl apply
# create from multiple files
kubectl apply -f ./my1.yaml -f ./my2.yaml

# start a single instance of nginx
kubectl create deployment nginx --image=nginx

# List a particular deployment
kubectl get deployment my-dep

# List all pods in all namespaces
kubectl get pods -wide --all-namespaces  --show-labels

# Get a pod's YAML
kubectl get pod my-pod -o yaml

# List pods Sorted by Restart Count
kubectl get pods --sort-by='.status.containerStatuses[0].restartCount'

# Get all running pods in the namespace
kubectl get pods --field-selector=status.phase=Running

# get the documentation for pod manifests
kubectl explain pods
kubectl describe pods my-pod

# Describe commands with verbose output
kubectl describe nodes my-node

# List PersistentVolumes sorted by capacity
kubectl get pv --sort-by=.spec.capacity.storage
```

```
# Retrieve the value of a key with dots, e.g. 'ca.crt'
kubectl get configmap myconfig \
  -o jsonpath='{.data.ca\.crt}'

# List Events sorted by timestamp
kubectl get events --sort-by=.metadata.creationTimestamp

# Compares the current state of the cluster
# against the state that the cluster would be in if the manifest was applied.
kubectl diff -f ./my-manifest.yaml

# Updating resources
# Force replace, delete and then re-create the resource. Will cause a service  ↩
    outage.
kubectl replace --force -f ./pod.json

# Create a service for a replicated nginx,
# which serves on port 80 and connects to the containers on port 8000
kubectl expose rc nginx --port=80 --target-port=8000

# Add a Label
kubectl label pods my-pod new-label=awesome

# Add an annotation
kubectl annotate pods my-pod icon-url=http://goo.gl/XXBTWq

# Auto scale a deployment "foo"
kubectl autoscale deployment foo --min=2 --max=10

# Edit the service named docker-registry
kubectl edit svc/docker-registry

# Scaling resources
kubectl scale --replicas=3 rs/foo                                # Scale a  ↩
    replicaset named 'foo' to 3
# Scale a resource specified in "foo.yaml" to 3
kubectl scale --replicas=3 -f foo.yaml

# Delete a pod using the type and name specified in pod.json
kubectl delete -f ./pod.json

# Delete pods and services with label name=myLabel
```

```
kubectl delete pods,services -l name=myLabel

# stream pod container logs (stdout, multi-container case)
kubectl logs -f my-pod -c my-container

# Run pod as interactive shell
kubectl run -i --tty busybox --image=busybox -- sh

# Attach to Running Container
kubectl attach my-pod -i

# Run command in existing pod (multi-container case)
kubectl exec my-pod -c my-container -- ls /

# Listen on port 5000 on the local machine and forward to port 6000 on my-pod
kubectl port-forward my-pod 5000:6000

# Show metrics for a given pod and its containers
kubectl top pod POD_NAME --containers
# Show metrics for a given node
kubectl top node my-node

# Mark my-node as unschedulable
kubectl cordon my-node
# Mark my-node as schedulable
kubectl uncordon my-node

# Drain my-node in preparation for maintenance
kubectl drain my-node

# If a taint with that key and effect already exists, its value is replaced as  ↩
    specified.
kubectl taint nodes foo dedicated=special-user:NoSchedule

# All namespaced resources
kubectl api-resources --namespaced=true
# All non-namespaced resources
kubectl api-resources --namespaced=false

# Access raw api
kubectl get --raw /apis/metrics.k8s.io/v1beta1
```

Chapter 10

Index

A
Apache Cassandra, 58
api-server, 20

C
CA, 47
chart, 40
Cluster Autoscaler, 47
ClusterIP, 8
ClusterRole, 69
ClusterRoleBinding, 69
ConfigMap, 79
Container Runtime Interface, 23
context, 70
controller-manager, 20
CRI, 23
cronjobs, 78

D
DaemonSet, 15
Dashboard UI, 36
Deployment, 5

E
Endpoints controller, 20
etcd, 20

H
Headless Service, 58
headless service, 58
HELM, 40
Helm, 40
Horizontal Pod Autoscaler, 43
HPA, 43

I
Identity, 69
Ingress, 12
Ingress Controller, 12
Ingress controller, 12
introduction, 1

J
Job, 76

K
kind, 21

L
Label, 15
label Selectors, 16
labels, 16
LoadBalancer, 11

M
MetalLB, 30
metrics server, 43
minikube, 21

N
Namespace, 70
namespace, 31
Node, 3
Node controller, 20
NodePort, 10

O
ordered pod creation, 62
Ordered Pod Termination, 68
Overprovisioning, 47

P
PersistentVolume, 50
PersistentVolumeClaim, 50
Pod, 2
pod, 2
pod network, 27
Pods network address space, 9
Pods ReplicaSets, 5
provisioner, 51
PV, 50
PVC, 50

R
RBAC, 69
ReplicaSet, 4
Replication controller, 20
Role, 69
Role-Based Access Control, 69
RoleBinding, 69

S
scheduler, 20
secret, 82

Secrets, 82
Selector, 15
Service, 8
Service Account & Token controllers, 20
Service accounts, 69
stateful application, 57
StatefulSets, 14
stateless application, 57
Storage, 49
Storage Classes, 50

V
volume plugin, 51
volumeClaimTemplates, 64
volumeMounts, 49
volumes, 49

W
wavenet, 27

Y
YAML, 16

About the author

Benjamin Young is the owner of www.comrite.com, an information technology consulting firm based in Austin, TX, specialized in software development (machine/deep learning, voip, web development etc). He has more than 20 years experience in software engineering, system/network administration.

He can be reached at: benjamin@comrite.com

Or by visiting:

http://amazon.com/author/benjaminyoung

https://github.com/mingewang/

AND PLEASE ...

If you find this book useful, I'd really appreciate a review (no matter how short) on amazon:

https://www.amazon.com/dp/B08HQTM57N/

This will help me continue to write quality books.

Other books by Benjamin Young:

- Docker for Dummies in Real World:
  https://www.amazon.com/dp/B06Y295S49/

- Pytorch Deep Learning By Example:
  Vol.1: https://www.amazon.com/gp/product/B08JKQLB8Z
  Vol.2: https://www.amazon.com/gp/product/B08JKPS7N5

- Deep Learning with Keras from Scratch: https://www.amazon.com/gp/product/1091838828/

www.ingramcontent.com/pod-product-compliance
Lightning Source LLC
Chambersburg PA
CBHW080849220526
45467CB00008B/2437